THE STORY OF
RAF HIXON

**A typical crew in training at RAF Hixon in 1944
with Vickers Wellington Twin-Engine Bomber KD-W**

*Photo from Navigator Flt Sgt Ken Stott from Welshpool,
who is in the centre of this fine photograph.*

Front Cover

**Vickers Wellington training aircraft lined up at RAF Hixon in 1943
Painting by Alan Preece based on original photograph. The painting hangs today in the offices of Hixon Airfield
Services, based in the former control tower.**

THE STORY OF
RAF HIXON

No. 30 OPERATIONAL TRAINING UNIT 1942–1945

Malcolm Garner

THE CHOIR PRESS

First published in the United Kingdom in 2022 by

The Choir Press

ISBN 978-1-78963-311-5

Contents

Foreword

It may be strange to begin a foreword with an apology, but I very much regret that this book was not completed twenty years ago. This is because, sadly, many of the people who had been alive during the lifetime of RAF Hixon, and who I interviewed in the 1990s, will by now have passed away and will not be able to read this history for themselves.

The apology is therefore for them.

As so often happens, a busy life gets in the way and with all the demands of work, family, moving house etc., I never managed to find the time to sit down and condense all the information and interviews into written form.

That was until 2020 – and Lockdown!

Being forced to remain at home and unable to travel, meet people etc. during Lockdown meant that at last I did have the opportunity to 'get the job done'. This book is the result.

I have felt privileged to have met so many fine people with their memories, be they villagers who lived through the wartime years of change, or those who worked or trained at RAF Hixon in the few years when it was working at full capacity to meet the demands of the war.

As I hope will be evident to the reader, the building of the training airbase of RAF Hixon had a profound and permanent influence on the geography of the village of Hixon, with the physical remains being converted to industrial or agricultural use and providing many people with an ongoing place of employment.

What is not so easy to appreciate today are the social and personal changes that took place at the time, and the sacrifice and commitment which was made by so many people, many from overseas, which contributed to victory in the Second World War.

Although this book does not attempt to be a full history of RAF Hixon, it is hoped the detail provided will help explain and preserve some of the more personal connections and memories of this momentous period.

Malcolm Garner

May 2022

CHAPTER ONE

Hixon and the Second World War

Introduction

Most people living and/or working in Hixon will know that there was once a Second World War airbase there, if only because they will know that the local industrial centre is called 'Airfield Industrial Estate'. Many, however, will have little knowledge of what lies behind that name and, today, most of the physical remains of the airbase and its activity are being obliterated with the passage of time and development.

The four large aircraft hangars for example, which remained unchanged and in place for many years, have now been rebuilt for alternative industrial use and are no longer readily recognisable. Similarly, the remains of the long concrete runways are less obvious, as some parts have been dug up and other parts are covered by hundreds of vehicles, some for scrapping, others for resale.

This brief book seeks to provide an introduction to the history of the airbase when it was in operation as RAF Hixon, from 1942–1945, and to provide details of the airbase infrastructure and operation, and of some of the thousands of men and

Airfield Industrial Estate Entrance Sign

women who were either based here, or came here to be trained to fly in active service with Bomber Command in the Second World War.

Although no bombs ever fell on Hixon, and it is probable that its sirens never sounded warning of an actual air raid, Hixon did make a major contribution to the war effort. The village and the airbase were well away from the coast and from the enemy, and the distance meant that it was never actually in the frontline. Nonetheless, the Second World War undoubtedly led to greater long-term changes to the village of Hixon than to many other places closer to the action.

Sad to say, it is also true that very many, if not most, of the brave airmen who trained at Hixon subsequently lost their lives in action. It is therefore appropriate that their commitment and sacrifice should be remembered and celebrated and it is hoped this book will help to make the story of RAF Hixon, and of some of the people who were based there, better known.

A number of villagers from Hixon had of course fought in the First World War, and some who lost their lives in that conflict are commemorated by plaques in the village hall. The hall itself was built

One of the four Type T2 Aircraft Hangars

after the First World War and is properly and appropriately known as Hixon Memorial Hall. Despite this more personal involvement in the First World War, the village of Hixon remained a relatively small and quiet agricultural community. The population had remained fairly steady since the early nineteenth century, at just over 300 people, and there seemed little reason to expect this to change when the Second World War started.

Change was on the way, however. Eighteen months after the war had started, in May 1941, a sign was planted in the ground close to the junction of New Road (then known as Station Road) and the present A51, announcing that the site had been chosen by the RAF for a new training airfield, or Operational Training Unit (OTU).

Hixon was probably chosen for a number of reasons. It was far enough away from the south and east coasts to be more secure from enemy air attack, yet within range of France and Germany for attack purposes when necessary. It had a large area of level ground, limited residential development and only low hills around it.

Soon after the announcement, workmen from 'Trollope and Cole', a Wolverhampton-based contractors, moved in and then started a period of frantic building activity. Local resident Dorothy Jenkinson, who lived at Wychdon Cottages, remembered the airfield being built with:

> *'lots of coaches bringing the large labour force in every day and people working furiously on the project.'*

The change for the people of Hixon was considerable and it must at times have seemed as though they had their own invasion.

Amerton

Stowe Village

Wychdon Cottages

Hixon Village

View of Airfield looking North (c.1990)

One important element of the construction work was the connection of services and drains to the airbase and Dorothy recalled the fact that the workmen's hut at the bottom of their garden (which backed onto the airfield) had running water whereas their own house still had to draw water from the garden well.

Among those involved in construction was Bill Chellingworth, an electrician from Gnosall. He had been working for the Air Ministry at Didcot but was recalled in 1942 and posted to Hixon to help build the airfield. He recalled that:

> *'It was a complete shambles when I arrived and for the first week I had to work in a hut that had been converted into a post office with a corporal in charge.'*

It might be thought that constructing an airfield is primarily a case of building the runways. In fact, developing the associated infrastructure was probably an even bigger task as accommodation and training facilities had to be provided for the workforce and trainee crews. These together eventually totalled well over 3,000 people!

Construction of the three runways in the usual triangular arrangement was nonetheless a major undertaking in its own right. The main No. 1 Runway stretched from the railway line at Hixon to Stowe village and was 4,750 feet long. No. 2 Runway ran from east to west and was 4,200 feet long, while No. 3 Runway was the shortest at 3,300 feet in length. Each was 50 yards wide and was built from concrete 6 inches thick. The three runways alone therefore required the mixing and laying of more than 34,000 cubic yards of concrete.

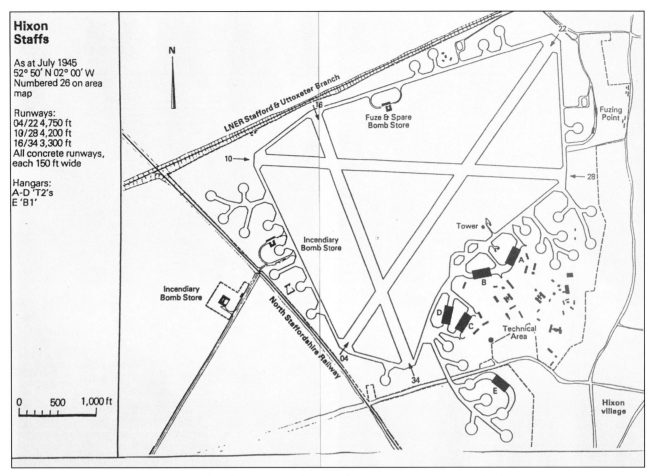

Wartime RAF Map of Airfield showing layout of runways, perimeter tracks, hangars etc.

In addition to the runways, perimeter tracks were constructed around the edge of the airfield at a standard 50 feet width with 30 feet clearance on each side. Thirty circular dispersal bays were sited at intervals around the perimeter track to allow the aircraft to be spread out away from buildings and one another, in case of air attack.

Further away still, for the same obvious reasons, were the two bomb stores. The main store near Amerton was of Type D and could store 200 tons of high explosive. The other near Shirleywich was smaller and used for storing incendiary bombs.

For similar reasons the many associated buildings were spread out around the locality. The main areas of building, some of which are shown on the accompanying maps, consisted of:

Technical area	Hangars, watch tower
Instructional site	Training buildings etc.
Communal site	Officers mess, communal dining room, gymnasium, church
WAAF communal site	WAAF officers mess and quarters
Dispersed residential sites No. 1 – 10	Officers' and airmens' sleeping quarters

WAAF dispersed site	Airwomens' sleeping quarters
Sick quarters (Egg Lane)	Hospital and ambulance garage
Sewage works	Sewage disposal & bucket cleaning plant

In total, the official (formerly secret) RAF map of the airbase gives details of over 350 separate buildings. These included the giant hangars, the watch office (control tower) and a huge variety of smaller but no less essential buildings.

The numerous accommodation buildings on the ten separate dispersed residential sites were mainly of the Liang or Nissen types. The former were built from timber, felt and plasterboard while the famous Nissen huts were of corrugated iron on a steel frame. Blast shelters of concrete were also built at each site while most of the other buildings were of temporary brick construction, actually a single thickness of bricks with a cement render. They were designed for a life of ten years and although most have now gone a few are still in use as industrial units some seventy-five years later.

Finding places to put all these buildings meant spreading well beyond the airfield itself with the result that many buildings were not only erected close to the village of Hixon, but also in much of the surrounding district.

The airfield layout was cleverly designed to minimise the impact on the existing village infrastructure but some demolition of existing property proved necessary. The main airfield area was formerly known as Amerton Heath and the farm of that name was entirely destroyed in the building operation. A small number of other buildings also had to be demolished as they could present a potential hazard to low-flying aircraft using the runways for take-off and landing. One such was 'Wychdon Villa', which was on the north side of Station Road soon after the railway level crossing. This property was directly in line with, and close to the end of, the shorter north-south No. 3 Runway and there was no alternative but to demolish it.

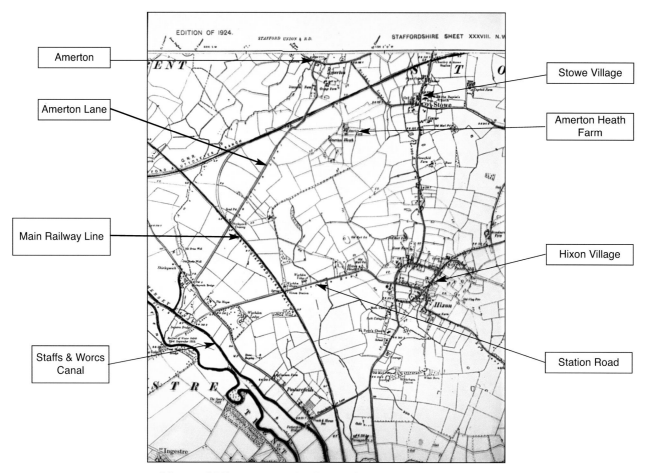

Map of Hixon area before airbase construction

Amerton

Amerton Lane

Main Railway Line

Staffs & Worcs Canal

Stowe Village

Amerton Heath Farm

Hixon Village

Station Road

Map of Hixon Area after airbase construction

Airbase Area Shown in Yellow

Shorter Runways

Ammunition Store

Wychdon Cottages

Wychdon Lodge

Ammunition Store

Main No. 1 Runway

Control Tower

Training Buildings

RAF Hospital

Accommodation Blocks

Another property that had to go was a large house on the east side of Stowe Lane where now stands the house known as Stowefields. Although further away from the east-west No. 2 Runway, this too was in line of take-off and landing, and had to be demolished. Most of the dozens of other new RAF buildings were however constructed on what we now call 'green field sites' in and around the village.

Another 'casualty' of the construction was a minor road called 'Amerton Lane'. This used to run from Shirleywich on the present A51 to Amerton on the A418 and had to be permanently closed. This was because the lane ran right across the north-west corner of the airfield and close to the end of the main No. 1 Runway. *(Interestingly the remaining stub ends of Amerton Lane can still be seen at Shirleywich and Amerton.)*

The speed of construction of the airbase was astonishing. Despite work only having started early in 1941, it was opened as a fully operational airbase in June 1942.

Wellington bomber and crew at RAF Hixon

The scale of this remarkable achievement may be gauged by the fact that by the end of 1942 no less than 2,800 people were living and working at the airbase – nearly ten times the total population of the village of Hixon itself.

Having managed to get the airfield 'up and running' in such a short time, the airfield and the village of Hixon were then the scene of three and a half years of frantic activity when No. 30 OTU, RAF Hixon, became the temporary or permanent home to many thousands of service personnel.

During this period there was rarely a time when the peace of the area was not shattered by the roar of the Bristol Hercules engines of the Wellington bombers based at the unit and used for training purposes, or the sight and sound of RAF personnel moving about the area, drinking in the village pubs or attending dances in the local village halls.

Thus, although the airbase was never itself attacked, with all the noise and activity, and hundreds of people in service uniforms, there was no doubt that the war had come to Hixon.

It is fortunate that in the 1990s, some fifty years later, a good number of people who had been at Hixon during the war agreed to be interviewed and their recollections recorded. They included people who were engaged in building the aerodrome, others who were based there as instructors, trainees or in other capacities, and also local villagers who had seen the remarkable changes that had been made to their environment.

What follows in this book are details of some of the events in Hixon during this period, based in no small part on these interviews and the first-hand memories of some of those who were there at the time.

CHAPTER TWO

RAF Hixon – No. 30 Operational Training Unit

What was an operational training unit?

In the early years of World War Two the casualty rate in Bomber Command was desperately high and there was an increasingly severe shortage of trained aircrew. The RAF therefore decided, as quickly as possible, to establish a number of 'operational training units' (OTUs) to meet the urgent need for additional aircrew and, more specifically, aircrew trained to undertake night-bombing operations over enemy territory.

Operational training units were built in various parts of the country and RAF Hixon became No. 30 OTU. It was established as a 'daughter' station of RAF Lichfield (27 OTU) and the first staff to be based at Hixon transferred from Lichfield to help get it 'up and running' in 1942. As mentioned in Chapter One the speed of construction was such that, within a year of construction starting, nearly 3,000 personnel were based at the airbase, some as instructors, some as ground and maintenance staff, others on a more short-term basis undertaking a period of training.

Who came there and what did they do?

The aircrew who came for training at Hixon were not trained from scratch here. Rather they had already completed training elsewhere for the different roles they would fulfil. They therefore arrived, having already trained and qualified as either pilots, navigators, gunners, wireless operators or bomb aimers at other training centres, sometimes overseas.

At an OTU like RAF Hixon these various differently trained airmen came to team up and form a crew who would then train together and learn to work in unison. As well as people from within the UK many airmen came from Commonwealth countries to support the cause and there were numerous airmen from New Zealand, Australia, South Africa and Canada who spent time training at RAF Hixon.

Bomber Crew at Hixon.
Sgt David Fellowes, Rear Gunner (front left)

Forming a Crew

It might seem remarkable now, but no directive was given regarding the formation of crews. Rather it was left to the individual airmen to make their own decisions as to who they should team up with to form a complete crew.

David Fellowes from Haywards Heath came to Hixon in 1943, having already trained as a rear gunner. He described the process of 'crewing up':

'There seemed to be no prior arrangement as to how crews would form. On arrival at Hixon people just got together in one big room and decided who they thought would "get on" with who. I had met an Australian pilot on the train, and we decided to stick together. We found an Australian wireless operator next and then looked around for a navigator. We thought a navigator should be good at maths, so we chose someone who looked studious! He was a Yorkshireman and was a good choice as he proved a very reliable navigator. In addition, we found a Scottish bomb aimer and a mid-upper gunner from London to complete what was a truly international crew!'

Wellington KD W with crew in training, photographed at Hixon in 1944
Sgt Ken Stott (Navigator) from Welshpool and crew

The system generally seemed to work well. It meant that people made their own choices and, as their lives could well depend on one another, it was very important they could work in harmony. The system was not infallible, however, and occasionally there were difficulties.

John Cooper from Stafford had this unfortunate experience. He was an air gunner and after training at RAF Seighford (a 'daughter' station of RAF Hixon), undertook three operational sorties from RAF Swinderby in Vickers Wellington aircraft. He recalled that:

'Our first navigator was not good at his job and on returning from one trip he announced that he thought we were over the Humber estuary. The rest of the crew were doubtful about this and this doubt turned to certainty when we found we were flying up the Thames and into an air raid over London! We beat a hasty retreat and headed up the coast and back to base. The navigator was removed from his post, but this meant that the rest of us in the crew had to return, this time to Hixon, to retrain with a new navigator.'

Happily, the new navigator proved more reliable, and the crew successfully completed a 'tour of operations' with 550 Squadron based at North Killingholme in Lincolnshire.

OTU training programme

After 'crewing up' the initial training pattern at an OTU was for ground instruction with lectures for the different disciplines, navigation, bomb aiming etc. in the training buildings.

Squadron Leader Ralph Edwards DSO, in his autobiography *In The Thick Of It*, describes being promoted to Flight Lieutenant and put in charge of the Instructional Fuselage Section of Ground Training at RAF Hixon in 1942. He explains:

'Our duties were to familiarise newly arrived trainee pilots with the 'Wellington' aircraft with the aid of two skeleton fuselages. As well as teaching engine handling, power settings for different attitudes and altitudes, speeds for take-off, climbing, cruising and landing etc, it was vitally important to make sure they were thoroughly conversant with all the emergency procedures and drills, such as where parachutes and dinghy were stowed, where the exits were located and the order of leaving the aircraft.'

One typical trainee, Sgt Tom Pegg from the USA, trained as a navigator and was posted to an OTU which had a similar training pattern to that at Hixon. He was instructed on Wellington Mark III and X and passed in the following areas:

- Baling out drill
- Ditching and dinghy drill
- Oxygen drill
- Procedure when lost at night
- SBA (Standard Beam Approach)
- Fire drill
- Petrol and oil systems

Achieving a pass in the second category proved rather difficult as he could not swim! Roy Norris from Oregon in USA explained how Tom and his crew overcame this in ingenious fashion.

'He lied that he could swim four lengths. This was not checked and so he proceeded with training. Part of ditching drill involved jumping from the top board of the baths into the pool with flying kit on. He managed to do this and get to the side but later he and his crew had to swim, with kit on, and get into an inflatable dinghy in the middle of a larger pool. He knew he couldn't do this but his supportive crew came up with a good idea to help out. One of them suggested it would be more realistic if they had to drag an injured airman with them and get him into the dinghy. The officer in charge thought this was a very good idea and, when asked for a volunteer, they all chose Tom! Thus it was that he got away as a non-swimmer and became part of a successful bomber crew!'

Crew members also had to pass decompression tests. These involved entering a decompression chamber using oxygen masks to simulate high altitude flying. The masks were then removed for a short period and the airmen's ability to cope with a lack of oxygen was assessed. A certificate was added to the person's log book once passed. New flying clothing was issued and then flying training could commence.

The aircraft most commonly based at Hixon for use in training were Vickers Wellington twin-engine bomber aircraft. They were not new aircraft and had usually seen active service and been replaced by more modern or more powerful and larger aircraft such as the Avro Lancaster. As a consequence, the planes at an OTU like Hixon were not always reliable or in good condition.

The first period of flying training was undertaken during the daytime and in company with an instructor. The instructors at OTUs were themselves experienced airmen who had completed their own 'tour of operations' (30 sorties) and were then 'screened' from further active service and posted to an operational training unit to pass on their experience.

As a result, several of those who did their initial training at Hixon later returned as instructors. This might be thought of as a comparatively easy task after the frightening experience of real bombing missions, but it was not always so. Many of the aircrew in training had only limited actual previous experience of flying, and mistakes and accidents were quite commonplace. Ken Tweedie from Queensland was at RAF Hixon as a navigation instructor and wrote to say:

'I flew three times with trainee aircrews in 1944 – a most frightening experience. Luckily after that I didn't have to fly again!'

Bill Hickox from Castle Donnington in Derbyshire was also a navigation instructor and was based at Hixon from October 1942 to March 1943. He recalled one particularly difficult flight when he was their instructor:

'On the whole the student navigators were quite good but on one occasion a pilot, who was supposedly an ex-Battle of Britain pilot, turned up for the briefing before the night flight smelling of ale! The crew were keen to go anyway and said that he could "take his drink" and it was the last flight they had to do before completing their course. Foolishly as it turned out, I agreed to give this a go. Once we were out towards the Irish Sea the radio on the Wellington failed completely, which meant we had to abort the flight and turn back to base immediately. This was now before the effects of any alcohol had time to wear off and as a result the pilot needed three attempts to land, and I remember being very cross about this. In the event the crew had to repeat the flight the following day and I can remember giving the crew a tremendous ticking off and telling them they must make sure they kept the pilot sober!'

Fighter affiliation: Miles Martinet making a mock attack on a Vickers Wellington at RAF Hixon

Picture drawn by John Teasdale in August 1943

After dual flying under instruction the crew then went 'solo', undertaking a range of different training activities to simulate conditions they were likely to experience when fighting the enemy. These included feathering propellers and single-engine flying, repeated take-offs and landings (known as circuits and bumps), flapless landings, formation flying and fighter affiliation. In fighter affiliation they would have to practice manoeuvres to avoid fighter aircraft. Several fighter aircraft were based at Hixon for this purpose with Curtiss Tomahawks, Hawker Hurricanes and others acting as the enemy.

Later the aircrews undertook bombing practice at both high and low levels on practice ranges. There were several local bombing ranges in use, the nearest being in Sherbrook Valley on Cannock Chase and another at Bagot's Park near Abbots Bromley. Remains of these can still be seen on Cannock Chase where the large target circle visible in the accompanying wartime photograph was made of broken white pottery sourced from the potteries in Stoke on Trent. It is still possible to find bits of pottery on the ground today, as well as seeing small depressions all around, the remains of bomb craters.

Another important element of the training course were cross-country flights. These would usually be at 15,000 feet or above, would last for up to 6 hours and would cover an equivalent distance to a flight to France or Germany. The routes taken from Hixon varied but a typical example was that of 4 March 1943 when Flight Lieutenant Steve Boylan (Pilot Instructor) took a crew in Vickers Wellington Mk10 (LN 406) on a cross-country flight lasting 4 hours 45 minutes. Their route was Hixon – Newmarket – Goole – St Ives – Fakenham – Peterborough – Hixon.

Bombing target

Sometimes cross-country flights would be combined with bombing practice to simulate a real raid. Steve Boylan's log book for April 19 1943 records one such flight. They flew from Hixon – Lake Vyrnwy – Rhyl – St Bee's Head (Cumbria) – Mull of Galloway – St Tudwal's Island (Llyn Peninsula) – Fishguard – Hixon, then bombed the target on Cannock Chase on their return. This flight lasted 5 hours 20 minutes.

Wartime photo of bombing range on Cannock Chase

Having completed these practice flights and manoeuvres in daylight the crew then moved to undertake similar training but at night-time. The total course for a new crew lasted approximately three months and flying times were usually in the region of thirty daylight hours and forty-five night-time hours.

In many cases, when crews had nearly completed their training, they were given a 'taste' of the real thing by going on what were called 'nickel' raids over enemy territory. These were flights to drop propaganda leaflets, usually over French towns and cities. Although regarded as a safer activity, these could still be dangerous missions, and more than one aircraft from Hixon was lost on such a flight.

Curtiss Tomahawks used for fighter affiliation exercises

In 1942, not long after RAF Hixon had opened, there was a general shortage of planes and crews in front line squadrons and the OTUs sometimes sent aircraft to supplement front line squadrons on the big bombing raids over Germany and France.

Hixon was no exception and sent Wellingtons on the famous 'Thousand Bomber Raids' to Bremen and Essen on separate nights in September 1942. These flights were undertaken by instructors rather than trainees. They would have previously seen action and were often keen to 'have another go' at the enemy.

Inevitably intensive flying training with inexperienced trainee crews was a hazardous business and accidents did happen. Many were minor incidents which, although recorded in the station log book, *(see Appendix 1)* had no long-term adverse effect. All too often however the consequences were more serious, and records indicate that more than a hundred aircrew were killed while undergoing training and based at Hixon. Some were killed in crashes in or around the neighbourhood, others disappeared or crashed while on the 'cross-country' training flights that took them all over Britain.

The station log book from RAF Hixon is held in the Public Record Office at Kew and contains outline details of more than a hundred accidents. *(Further details of some of these are provided in Appendix 2.)*

After completing their training at Hixon, the crews either transferred directly to a squadron for frontline service or more commonly, later in the war when more powerful aircraft were in use, to a Heavy Conversion Unit. At the HCU the crew would undergo further training on the type of aircraft they would fly on operations, usually Lancaster bombers. From there they would be posted to a squadron for their 'tour of operations', usually thirty missions over enemy territory.

Sadly, the loss rate amongst bomber crews was very high. It is salutary to realise that, in all probability, most of the airmen who trained at Hixon were subsequently killed in action.

Bryce Chase, a pilot from Saskatchewan who trained at Hixon from May to July 1943, recalled that:

'Of the ten crews from my course who were posted to squadrons in England, nine were lost in action.'

Overall, Bomber Command suffered terrible losses with more than 57,000 crew killed during the war and over 8,300 planes lost in action. However, against this must be placed the remarkable achievements of Bomber Command and the major contribution they made to limiting Germany's manufacturing capability and therefore the winning of the war. Airmen trained at RAF Hixon played a significant part in helping to achieve this success.

Graves of four overseas airmen in St Peter's Churchyard, Hixon – All were killed while in training at RAF Hixon

CHAPTER THREE

Living Alongside the RAF in Hixon – Villagers' Experiences

Until the war had been underway for a couple of years, it seems likely that the villagers of Hixon would have thought of it as a somewhat remote event, apart from the probable departure of some of the younger citizens to take an active role in one of the armed services.

All this changed from spring 1941 when construction of the airbase started. Suddenly there would have been hundreds of workers arriving by the coachload every day and re-shaping the triangle of land between the village and the railway to the east, and between Hixon and Stowe to the north.

One new arrival, not a villager but someone who was posted to Hixon during construction, recalled that:

> *'Station Road (now New Road) was just a narrow lane and quite unsuitable for the heavy traffic that would be needed for the air base. McAlpine's were brought in to upgrade the road to take heavy vehicles.'*

As mentioned earlier, one farm was completely obliterated, and two properties had to be demolished because they were in line with the new runways and would have been a danger to aircraft taking off and landing. One other property which was nearly in line with a runway was Wychdon Lodge on Station (New) Road. This house, which still stands today, was thought to be far enough away not to be a hazard to aircraft. Sadly, this decision was a mistake and, as is described in Chapter Five (Accidents and Incidents), led to the deaths of six airmen in 1944 when it was hit by their plane in difficulties during take-off.

Some airmen and ground staff found lodgings with local villagers. George Riley, for example, lodged happily with Frank and Doris Northover on Stowe Lane. He enjoyed village life and recalled that Betty Blewer, who ran a pig farm on Back Lane, used to collect the leftover food from the base to use as pigswill. Many airmen and residential staff made good use of the local pubs, though George Riley commented that:

> *'I used to avoid the 'Bank House' as there always seemed to be a lot of fights there!'*

The 'Green Man' and 'The Cock' at Stowe were others used regularly, as was the village hall where dances were held. Other pubs were the 'Hollybush' at Salt, the 'Coach & Horses' at Pasturefields and the 'Clifford Arms' at Great Haywood

One villager who came closer to the action than she would have wanted was Dorothy Jenkinson. She lived at one of the Wychdon Cottages, which still stand beside the railway today. She had moved there in 1942 and at that time there was no water, electricity, gas or sanitation. Ironically, although her own house had no running water supply, the workmen's huts in the field behind the house did have water 'on tap'.

She remembered a number of accidents, and one in particular, where an aircraft overshot the runway and landed in the spinney at the end of their garden. Dorothy was in the tin bath in front of the fire at the time!

She recalled that the guard on duty at the crash site gave her some parachute silk from which she made tops for her boys.

Wychdon Cottages today, with airfield behind – the level crossing was in the foreground, at the fence

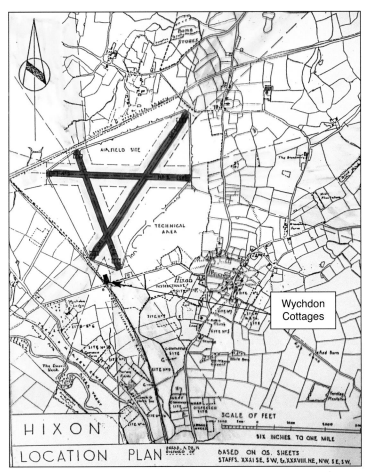

Map to show flight paths (in yellow) for each of the three runways and the position of Wychdon Cottages (in black) beside the railway level crossing and between No. 1 and No. 3 Runways

A little further along the railway line from the cottages were the shooting butts, the firing range for small arms and for testing aircraft guns. Dorothy remembered the bullets often missed the target and on occasions they could hear them sailing over the house. This was stopped when Mr Elsmore next door complained. At the time Hixon Station was still open and Mr Elsmore worked the level crossing gates.

Situated right at the end of her garden was one of the many 'dispersal' bays. These were circular concrete pads spaced around the airfield perimeter track where aircraft would be parked and serviced between flights. *(Note: dispersal bays were spaced apart so that, in the event of an enemy attack, it would be more difficult to damage aircraft than if they were parked closer together.)*

Dorothy recalled that:

'On one occasion when a plane was parked, I didn't notice that my baby son had run away up the garden and through the hedge. When I noticed he was gone I saw him standing underneath a Wellington bomber, right by the wheel! I was frantic with worry and raced down the garden only to find two

of the airmen calmly talking to him. After that incident, my brother-in-law came and laid the hedge to block any holes to avoid a repetition.'

Dorothy used to put up airmen's wives when they were visiting their husbands who were based at Hixon. She remembered one memorable occasion when:

A Wellington bomber being serviced in the open air, parked on a dispersal bay *(artist unknown)*

'A pilot's wife was staying when her husband went on a night raid from Hixon to Germany. His wife was extremely anxious and persuaded me to stay with her in the bedroom, in the same bed, while her husband was on the raid because she was so frightened. Fortunately, he returned safely from the raid, but I can remember vividly having to get up in the middle of the night and leave the warm bed and go to my own room to make room for the pilot husband!'

It may seem amazing that people were able to live so close to the end of the main runway as Dorothy, especially with young children. Nonetheless Dorothy was remarkably sanguine and remarked that at least they could sleep in comfortable beds at night and were reasonably fed compared with the terrible suffering not so far away in Birmingham and Coventry.

Another villager, Joe Tinker, lived at Chartley Farm Cottages and was about ten years old when the war started. He remembered one night in the winter of 1943/44 when, at about 8 pm, the lights in the house all went out and there was a loud bang. It transpired that a Wellington bomber had crashed close to their cottage and demolished the overhead power cables to the house. It finished up about 150–200 yards away from the house and burst into flames. Most of the crew escaped but sadly the tail gunner was killed. As can be imagined such an experience left an indelible mark in the mind of a child, and Joe still remembered the incident vividly some fifty years later.

Another villager who witnessed a plane crashing and catching fire was Cyril Fradley. He was a baker and confectioner who worked in Weston Village but lived in Hixon, close to the airfield, in the row of houses in New Road on the left as you come into the village. Like all the locals during the war, Cyril got used to planes flying at all hours of the day and night and took little notice. However, on Thursday 10 February 1944, when he was returning home from collecting his two children from the local school just before 4 pm, he noticed that one plane – a Vickers Wellington – was having problems at about 4,000 feet and that there was trouble with the starboard engine which was making an unusual 'pop-popping' noise.

The day was bright but there was a strong wind blowing and as he watched he saw the plane lose height rapidly as the pilot attempted to make an emergency landing on the shorter north-south runway from the southern (New Road) direction.

Unfortunately, the pilot was unable to reach the runway and the plane crash-landed with its wheels down, in the field on the southern side of the road. The starboard wheels of the undercarriage were either retracted, or more likely collapsed, with the result that the aircraft veered to the right and collided with a large concrete mixer being used in construction work at the large B1 (Vickers) hangar *(the one on the right as you drive into Hixon).*

The B1 hangar to the right of Station (New) Road just before the Village – it was by this hangar that the plane crashed from which villager Cyril Fradley tried to rescue Sgt Welstead when the plane was on fire

Local Villager Cyril Fradley at Buckingham Palace having received the British Empire Medal for his bravery in attempting to save the life of a trapped airman in a burning crashed aircraft

Cyril saw all this happen and watched as the tail gunner escaped by way of his rear turret, as did a couple of the others, including the instructor, through a hatch. After a couple of seconds, however, flames started to spread from the port engine towards the cockpit. Another crew member, in trying to escape through the cockpit window, became trapped by his parachute harness and was left suspended on the side of the burning plane. Although the airman was surrounded by flames, Cyril Fradley ran to the plane and, at the second attempt, managed to drag him clear. In the process both he and the airmen, Sgt Arthur Welstead, received severe burns.

Sadly, Sgt Welstead succumbed to his injuries soon afterwards and Cyril Fradley was in hospital for several weeks recovering. Sgt Welstead was buried in Kennington Cemetery, close to his home.

For his brave action Cyril was awarded the British Empire Medal. He received this in person from King George VI at Buckingham Palace in October 1944. The letter of invitation to the investiture stated that he and his family could claim railway travelling expenses, but only third class!

As with Cyril Fradley and Dorothy Jenkinson, Hixon villagers would have become used to the almost constant noise of planes coming and going.

Careful records were kept of the total number of hours flown each month, during daylight and at night, by planes from RAF Hixon. These records, along with various other original documents, are now kept in the Public Record Office at Kew and are available for inspection by arrangement.

Remarkably, the records show that, in 1943 and 1944, during the spring and summer months when longer days meant more flying was possible, there was an average total every month of no less than 3,000 flying hours.

Simple maths shows that a month of thirty-one days only contains 744 hours (31×24). This means that at any one time, twenty-four hours per day, every day, there were at least four planes in the air at, or from, RAF Hixon.

Some of these would of course have been away on long cross-country flights, but there would often be others, circling round noisily, practising take-offs and landings (circuits and bumps).

All this would have been a big contrast from the peaceful village which Hixon would have been, only eighteen months earlier.

This level of activity was confirmed by John Teasdale from Stafford, then a fourteen-year-old schoolboy. He was a keen observer of aircraft movements and regularly visited Hixon between 1942 and 1944, keeping amazingly detailed notes. His log for August 1942 records that:

> *'Flying activity increased rapidly during August with up to four Wellingtons doing circuits and bumps and local flying at any one time!'*

John was also an extremely good artist, and the picture below was one of many he drew of the planes he observed at RAF Hixon during this period, several of which appear in this book.

Vickers Wellington as based at Hixon – picture drawn in 1944 by schoolboy John Teasdale

CHAPTER FOUR

RAF Hixon – Daily Life 'on the Ground' at the Airbase

Inevitably, in reviewing the history of RAF Hixon, the focus will tend to be on the airmen and on their flying training programme which was, after all, the 'raison d'etre' for the existence of No. 30 OTU.

However, there were many other staff based at RAF Hixon and aspects of organisation behind the scenes without which the training programmes could not be carried out safely or as quickly.

When the airbase was first established, in the early years of the war, there was a necessary focus on defence because at that stage there was always the possibility of invasion. With this in mind a clear directive went out stating that:

> 'Each airbase had to be able to defend itself against attack and airmen had to learn to use small arms to undertake this task.'

At the outset, several defence posts were established in the area. With the benefit of hindsight, it has to be said that there is an element of 'Dad's Army' about the locations chosen. These included the 'railway yard at Chartley Station', an 'Old Marl Pit near Stowe Crossroads' and one at 'Shirleywich level crossing'. Each of these was to be equipped with Sten guns, rifles, an Aldis lamp and a radio telephone set. There is also a reference to a Cyclist Fighting Patrol though no further details have been discovered.

As the war progressed it became clear that defence training was not very popular, probably because the likelihood of attack seemed remote. Consequently, this stern yet still faintly amusing warning was recorded in the station log book in October 1943:

> 'It should be remembered that men may well be called upon to defend themselves and their station and even a small party of men, all with flat feet and bad backs, who could use an automatic weapon might turn the tide against the enemy, so all medical chits (to be excused) must be subjected to careful scrutiny. It boils down to the fact that, whether we like it or not, defence training has to be and is going to be done.'

Whether this pronouncement had any effect is not recorded! Certainly, this is the final reference to it in the station log book.

Entertainment was also recognised as being important in maintaining and boosting morale and, rather remarkably, some entertainment was already on hand when the airbase opened. This was because, in the First World War, a local farmer called Wilmot Martin had established a travelling concert party with the initial intention of raising funds for the war effort. He had modelled himself on the famous Sir Harry Lauder, a music hall star and one of the best paid entertainers in the world. He sang the same songs and dressed in a similar manner, wearing a kilt, and holding a characteristic crooked walking stick. In this way Wilmot and members of the Hixon Concert Party raised many thousands of pounds and continued between the wars raising funds to, for example, buy shoes for local children and to pay for them to have an annual outing to the seaside.

The Hixon Concert Party with local farmer Wilmot Martin dressed in similar style to the famous concert hall star Harry Lauder and carrying a trademark crooked walking stick

Thus, in an extraordinary twist of fate, when the 'war came to Hixon' in 1942 the Hixon Concert Party were immediately available and were invited to perform at the local airbase to entertain the airmen and women in September 1942. They must have been well received for they were asked to do so again on several subsequent occasions in 1942 and 1943.

A station cinema was opened in August 1942 with twice weekly film shows, and an entertainment committee was established in October. The popular film shows were increased to thrice weekly and various dances and concerts were also organised, some in the Hixon Memorial Hall.

By May 1943 the popular cinema was re-equipped with two 35mm projectors and 'tip-up' seats, and films were now shown on six nights every week with the programmes changed every Monday and Thursday. As well as more frequent dances there were also occasional lectures and concerts.

One of the people who trained at Hixon, and later became very well-known, was radio broadcaster Cliff Michelmore CBE. He was invited to open the first Hixon History Society 'Wartime Years' Exhibition in 1992, but sadly was unable to come as he was filming in Canada. He nonetheless replied saying:

'As I pass by the level crossing at Hixon when I am on the train, I do give a glance across to what was the Officers' Mess, my Nissen hut and the airfield and village beyond. I'm sorry I cannot come to your event as I would have liked the excuse to do so. As you know Lord Aylstone was also there (ex-Labour Cabinet Minister, Chair of IBA etc.) as was Sir William Glock (BBC Controller of Music) who gave piano recitals to the WAAF – never to us!' (WAAF = Women's Auxiliary Air Force.)

The station log book does indeed record one piano recital by 'Flight Lieutenant Glock' on 1 October 1943, though it does not make mention of the gender of the audience!

Generally, RAF Hixon was regarded as a happy station by those who passed through the airbase, although some who, like the Australians, had come from warmer climes found the cold winter weather quite a challenge. Bill Gourlay (more details in Chapter Seven) wrote about the very cold winter of 1944/45 and the difficulty of keeping warm in the accommodation huts which each had just one wood-burning stove to stave off the cold. Fuel was in short supply and residents would occasionally supplement the 'ration' by dismantling wooden parts of the hut. Bill recalled one windy winter's day when everyone had gone into Stafford or to the camp cinema:

'On arriving "home" there was great astonishment to find that the hut was flat on the ground, collapsed like a pack of cards! Investigations next day revealed that the structure just had no collar ties at all to the rafters nor any cross joists tying the tops of the walls together! These timbers had all gone in the "worthy" cause of trying to feed the stove to keep warm!'

Both trainee crews and ground crew personnel made good use of local hostelries. Norman Lowe from Bolton was a sergeant armourer fitter who moved ammunition from the bomb stores then loaded these aboard the Wellingtons and bullets into the turrets. He remembered the social side being very lively with regular visits to the 'Lamb and Flag', 'Coach and Horses', 'Clifford Arms' and the 'Woolpack' all being on his regular itinerary.

Another Australian navigator who trained at Hixon, Ken Tweedie, remembered that on one occasion:

'Some members of the navigation section took a few coloured "Verey" cartridges apart and, climbing on the roof of the adjacent Nissen hut (signals section) dropped the cartridge "innards" down the flue of their stove – with very spectacular results!'

In thinking back to what life was like to be based at RAF Hixon, one aspect that is easily overlooked is the young age of both aircrew and ground staff. Many of the men and women were only in their early twenties and some even in their late teens.

Noel Burton for example had started training as a pilot in his home country of Rhodesia at the age of just eighteen. When posted to RAF Hixon in 1942 he was still only nineteen years old.

He was though, by then, a qualified pilot and this was a position of some importance. The pilot was the 'boss' of any crew yet, in his case, apart from the flight engineer, Noel was the youngest member of the seven-man crew. Despite his youth he proved an able pilot and leader, and after successfully completing a 'tour of ops' with 106 Squadron flying Lancasters, he returned to Hixon as an instructor, yet was still only twenty-one years old.

Another young pilot posted to RAF Hixon as an instructor was Flight Lieutenant Steve Boylan.

Bicycles were issued to airbase staff for transport – very few had learnt to drive a car or could afford one.
Photo from F/Sgt Terry Hillyer, Air Gunner, from Croydon (at left of photo)

He arrived in November 1942, also still aged only twenty-one years. Remarkably he had by then already completed a 'tour of ops' in the Middle East and had played a significant part in the defence of the island of Malta (something for which he was later awarded the Malta George Cross Fiftieth Anniversary Medal). He commented that:

> *'The young men I was training were usually aged between nineteen and twenty-three so I was more or less the same age as many of those I was training. Many of them came from countries all over the Commonwealth and I found them all to be enthusiastic and hard-working, never shirking any task.'*

As an aside, one other feature which would seem extraordinary today, especially in view of his flying experience and responsibility, was that Steve had not by this stage learnt to drive a car! He explained that:

> *'I could fly a plane long before I could drive a car. I recall one occasion when I was sitting in a van at the airbase but had no idea what to do!'*

He, like many other officers and service personnel, had to use a bicycle to get around the sprawling airbase at Hixon, rather than motorised transport.

A very grainy but unique photo showing the bar inside the Officers' Mess at RAF Hixon

Steve was one of a number of the airmen and personnel based at Hixon who met and later married their girlfriends. Ken Tweedie from Queensland was another. He had trained as a navigator and 'crewed-up' and trained at Hixon in 1943. After he had completed his 'tour of ops' with 460 Squadron (RAAF), Ken returned to Hixon as a navigation instructor. While back at the airbase Ken met a local Stafford girl – Rose Chilton from Tixall Road – and they married in 1944.

Another overseas airman, Pilot Officer Noel Burton from Rhodesia, also returned to Hixon as an instructor. On his return he met and became engaged to one of the WAAF based at Hixon, Leading Aircraft Woman (LACW) Barbara *(Bobbie)* Davies. She was a dental nurse and worked at one of the two dental surgeries opened on the airbase, probably in the old hospital building off Egg Lane. She was later promoted to Corporal, quite a rarity in the dental branch apparently.

Noel described one of their first dates – one that didn't start so well:

'On an early occasion when I first met my wife-to-be, I invited her to a village dance held in the hall about four miles away. Because I had no means of transport we had to walk. Bobbie, being very smartly dressed in uniform and having a comparatively new pair of shoes did not find me very comforting after the long walk and deserted me on arrival at the hall. Her friends accused her of being extremely rude to me, which made her think again and she re-joined the lonely soul sitting despondently on one of the benches. I managed to scrounge a lift back with a more well-to-do fellow officer, so we arrived back at the billet without further upset. This fortunately did not prevent us going out together more frequently.'

Their relationship fortunately survived this experience, and they became engaged. Their wedding was planned for 7 June 1944, but unexpectedly had to be brought forward to 17 May. Noel explained:

'We were not told why we had to change the date of our wedding at the time but found out later that it happened to be the date proposed for D Day and that it couldn't be cancelled in our favour!'

They returned to Rhodesia after the war and enjoyed fifty-five years of marriage until Bobbie sadly passed away. Noel was able to revisit Hixon in 2002 and enjoyed seeing again the surviving airfield buildings and the house in which he and Bobbie lodged after their wedding (High Cross in High Street).

Vickers Wellington aircraft and bomb trailers at RAF Hixon in 1943

There were of course many ground staff based at Hixon on a permanent basis, carrying out a variety of roles. One such was Deryck (Jack) Brew from Burntwood. He was a corporal armourer, tasked to arm the planes while the aircrew were being briefed.

He recalled one incident when they were using a Fordson Tractor to collect a fresh load of bombs from Weston Railway Station.

'Our tractor ran away when it was taken out of gear, and we were struggling to get it back into gear as it ran down the hill. Eventually we succeeded with the result that the tractor nearly stopped dead and the bombs all rolled off and fell into the ditch! We were all very anxious about this, but fortunately no one in authority noticed!'

Another member of ground staff based at RAF Hixon throughout its years of operation was Flight Sergeant Stan Botwright from Woking. He was a physical training instructor and his role, based at the gymnasium, was keeping RAF personnel fit, organising games such as football, cricket, hockey etc., and keeping aircrew occupied when the aircraft were grounded due to bad weather. On these occasions there were as many as 100–200 people to keep occupied, no small task!

He also worked with aircrew at Stafford Baths teaching and training them how to survive if their aircraft ditched at sea. Stan and his wife lived in Stafford rather than at Hixon and he remembered how 'cushy' he felt his job was at the baths, working from 0900–1200hrs then, after home lunch, from 1400–1600hrs.

A funeral service at St Peter's Church, Hixon for an overseas airman killed in training – airbase staff were called on to provide a guard of honour on such occasions

The work wasn't all fun and games, however, and he also recalled:

'sad times when aircrew were killed flying circuits and bumps and we were asked to provide the guard of honour at the funeral.'

Further details of one funeral procession can be found in Chapter Seven. This tells the story of Deryck Rowse who is buried at St Peter's Church in Hixon.

It is important to remember that it was not only men who were based at RAF Hixon. Although no women were trained as aircrew in those days, more than 400 members of the Women's Auxiliary Air Force (WAAF) were posted to the airbase. Members of the WAAF fulfilled a range of land-based roles including medical and dental duties, parachute packing, catering, meteorology, aircraft maintenance, and radar and telephone communications.

As with the airmen, most were young and inexperienced. George Riley, an experienced aerial photography instructor, arrived at Hixon in 1941, just as the airbase was opening. He remembered that:

> 'When the first WAAFs arrived, the place was an absolute shambles. The girls were collected from the railway station and, in those days of inequality, some of them were due to be waitresses in the officers' mess. All the beds for these WAAFs were un-erected and were in a huge pile together with another pile of sheets, three-piece mattresses, pillows etc. and the girls were simply shown the pile and told to put them up. Many of them were very upset by this lack of preparation and there were a lot of tears. Some of the men, including myself, took pity on them, told them to go away and then set to and put their beds together for them.'

One early member of the WAAF posted to Hixon was Beryl Spear. She had trained as a meteorologist and, after a five-week course in London, was posted to Hixon in September 1942. In a talk in 1988 to the Royal Meteorological Society, she described her experience:

> 'Conditions at Hixon were somewhat primitive. The WAAF site was a sea of mud and we lived in a Nissen hut with barely a foot between beds. The camp was "dispersed", which meant that it was at least a mile from our site to the cookhouse, and another mile or more to the airfield and "met office" on the ground floor of the watch office (control tower). When we were on the morning shift, we not only made our breakfast of tea and toast in the met office, but also washed in the little cloakroom as, usually, there was no hot water on the WAAF site.

> 'Our meteorological observations included temperature and pressure readings and weather conditions, but also estimates of cloud height. The latter could be quite a challenge. During the day, if the cloud was a layer of unknown height, we released a red balloon which went up at about 300 feet a minute and timed it until it entered the cloud. With no anemometer we had to estimate wind speed and direction – facing into the wind until it blew on both ears, the direction being where the nose was pointing!

> 'Estimating visibility was also something of a headache. Long before the Clean Air Act was in place smoke came from factories in every direction, Wolverhampton, Birmingham, the potteries etc. During my eight month stay at Hixon, I saw the seven-mile visibility point only once!'

Another female member of ground staff was WAAF Betty Jermy, formerly from Rugeley. She was a leading aircraft woman fitter 2E and was based at Hixon in 1944. She wrote:

> 'We were stationed on a small satellite site and it was there I celebrated my twenty-first birthday (18 June 1944.) Mum, Dad and a friend had given up rations so I could have a cake. It was a delicious fruit cake and we girls thoroughly enjoyed it as food was not short but not too appetising either on the camp.

> 'Our site was in a cornfield and the Nissen huts were overrun with little brown mice. They were everywhere and I woke, following my birthday celebrations, to find the remainder of my cake being eaten by several of the wee creatures despite having hung it on a string bag on a peg dangling over my bedspace. I was very naïve in those days and genuinely delighted in the sight of the mice. Having food in the billet was, by the way, breaking the rules.

> 'Nonetheless, every morning a fresh churn of milk was left at the field (site) gate for we girls to drink. It was so fresh and creamy – I hope someone at the time thanked the farmer.'

Curtiss Tomahawk taking off at RAF Hixon in snow – this is the only known photograph of a plane taking off or landing at RAF Hixon in wartime

A very dramatic incident recalled by Betty Jermy was when:

'A Wellington we were working on caught fire in the hangar and we all had to run for our lives – very frightening and dramatic! There was a Court of Enquiry following the fire and we were all called in turn to give our account. Fortunately, no one was hurt but we lost an aircraft.'

Deryck (Jack) Brew also remembered the incident and commented that:

'The heat from the fire was tremendous and the propellors of the plane started to turn simply from the hot air rising past them!'

David Starey from Stone was also there. He worked in Hangars 3 and 4, two of the T2 type hangars which stood in what is now the industrial estate. He was a leading aircraftsman responsible for mainframes and, being closer to events, was able independently to give a much more detailed account of what actually happened (probably on 20 November 1944 – see Appendix 1).

He explained that:

'We were encouraged to keep the floors of the hangars clear of oil and so on, and sometimes would be warned that some high official was coming to do an inspection and that we should "prepare the hangar" for this.

'In order to clean any oil off the surface of the hangar floor in Hangar 3, we would open the drain cocks on the fuel tanks under the wings and let the petrol run out over the floor and then be swept around. This was of course highly dangerous and unauthorised and led to a near disaster.

'On this occasion an officer came in to inspect the aircraft and stood under the wing and lit his cigarette with a lighter. As a result, the petrol ignited and, although nobody was killed or injured, the plane in the *hangar completely burnt out and the hangar itself was "white hot". There was ammunition on the plane which was going off and oxygen bottles also exploding.'*

It was a very dangerous incident, but the officer concerned managed to avoid court martial because he threatened, if court martialled, to reveal the fact that they were spreading petrol all over the floor and wasting Air Ministry fuel in order to clean the hangar. Amazingly he got away with it, but David remarked that:

'We had to shovel up the remains of that plane, so complete was the destruction.'

Remarkably the hangar survived intact and unchanged for many years after the war and has only recently been completely rebuilt for its current industrial use.

Another dramatic incident David Starey recalled was connected to the development by Vickers of an emergency air bottle for lowering the undercarriage of Wellington bombers. This invention was eventually successfully developed and was adopted as the standard for the whole of Bomber Command. He explained that:

'During trials, on one occasion, a Wellington was taken up and an attempt made to land using this emergency bottle. The attempt failed and the undercarriage did not come down with the result that the plane had to land on its belly. This test had not been authorised by the Air Ministry so in a rather hush-hush fashion, Vickers paid for the repair of this complete underbody section of the plane, and we had to carry out the work in Hangar 4. By working flat out on the job – which would normally have taken three months – we managed to complete it in one week!'

As mentioned at the beginning of this chapter, it is perhaps inevitable, in looking back at the RAF in wartime, that there is a focus on the actual flying and on bombing missions against the enemy.

Yet without an ongoing training programme, a substantial infrastructure and a hard-working and skilled workforce based at airfields in the UK, such direct action against the enemy would not have been possible.

The stories above give just a glimpse into these 'behind the scenes' activities and the debt of gratitude owed to the hundreds of people who provided this support.

Chapter Five

Accidents and Incidents at 30 OTU, RAF Hixon 1942–1945

The original station log book from RAF Hixon is lodged at the National Records Office at Kew near London, and is full of fascinating, though often brief, details regarding incidents and activities at the airbase throughout the war. (See Appendix 1 and 2.)

Many of these entries relate to mishaps or accidents and, during the period from September 1942 to January 1945, there are details of 141 accidents, with 33 of these involving fatalities. In all it is estimated that, tragically, well over 100 airmen lost their lives while in training at RAF Hixon.

While this is an awful statistic, and one that sounds extraordinarily high, it should be remembered that, over this period, there would have been tens of thousands of flights, at all times of day and night. The planes used in training were generally ones that had been retired from mainstream squadron operations and were often in poor condition. As a consequence, there were numerous instances where planes or their equipment failed, and flights had to be delayed or aborted.

Commonwealth War Graves in St Peter's Churchyard – these are the graves of airmen from overseas who were killed while in training at RAF Hixon

As mentioned earlier, many pilots and other aircrew were remarkably young and had limited previous experience. As such it is perhaps remarkable that the loss rate was not higher still and reflects great credit on the bravery and skill of aircrew and the efforts of ground maintenance staff.

Some of the records provide detail of more minor, even amusing incidents, such as the one on 9 October 1942 when:

'A Boulton and Paul Defiant 1, piloted by P/O Bartley, collided with a horse and cart while taxying.'

The record states that:

'The horse appeared bruised, and damage was caused to the leading edge of the starboard mainplane and one of the airscrew blades.'

It was not uncommon for planes landing towards the west on the main No. 1 Runway to fail to stop before the end then skid onto or even across the main London to Manchester Railway Line which ran across the end of the runway. The very first record in the log book, for Friday 11 September 1942, records one such incident, noting that:

'The aircraft was only slightly damaged and the only casualty, the air gunner, sustained minor cuts and slight shock.'

Similar things happened on numerous occasions and ground crew were specially assigned to retrieve planes using a range of equipment, including inflatable airbags, to bring the aircraft back to the hangars for repair.

Even the most patient of the 'crash crew' members might, however, have been exasperated on Saturday 26 August 1944. On that afternoon, at 1500hrs, one of Hixon's Wellington bombers overshot the runway and ran onto the railway line. Then no sooner had the ground crew recovered this plane that, at 2255hrs on the same day, another Wellington did exactly the same thing! Fortunately, the crews of both planes were uninjured.

So frequently did this happen that the London Midland & Scottish Railway Company installed new colour light signals both north and south of Hixon with a switch fitted in the RAF Control Tower which could change them, and the preceding signals, to red in an emergency. This was a most unusual arrangement but meant they could stop trains running immediately after an accident or during recovery operations.

Although there were numerous less serious accidents of this sort, sadly the log book also gives outline details of a number of more serious incidents in which lives were lost.

The first of these was on 31 October 1942, soon after the station became operational. The log book states that:

'Wellington (Z1083) was practising circuits with F/S Belgrove as the pilot and W/O Primrose as the instructor. At 2050hrs the plane stalled at 500 ft and crashed and burst into flames at Grange Farm, Amerton, adjacent to the northern boundary of the airfield. The crew of six were all killed.'

Two members of this crew, Flight Sergeants Hawk and Wooliams, both from Canada, are buried in St Peter's Churchyard, Hixon.

Only three months later there was another fatal accident, also involving crew members from the Commonwealth. This five-man crew were well on the way to completing their training course when, on Tuesday 7 February 1943, they were returning in their Vickers Wellington from a long cross-country training flight when the accident happened.

The Australian pilot, Bob Lewis, touched down on the main runway but for some reason decided to abort the landing and go round again. As the plane climbed away from the west end of the main runway, it stalled and crashed close to Ingestre Rectory, about a mile further west, killing all five men on board.

This photo was taken just a month before this crew were all killed in a flying accident at Hixon on
Tuesday 7 February 1943

Coming from overseas, Bob Lewis, and Air Gunner Deryck Rowse from New Zealand, were also buried in war graves at St Peter's Church in Hixon.

All the overseas airmen buried at St Peter's Church are commemorated on a plaque inside the church and their names are read aloud each year on Remembrance Sunday. The accompanying photo of the crew was taken just a month before their fatal crash. (Note: Please see Chapter Seven for further details of Deryck Rowse from New Zealand.)

Two months later, on 10 April 1943, another fatal crash occurred to a plane from Hixon, this time on a flight to practice night-time bomb aiming. After only twenty-five minutes in the air, and when over Derbyshire, the plane suffered an engine failure. As the other engine was already running rough, the pilot decided to attempt an emergency landing. He managed to do a 'wheels-up' landing on a straight section of main road at Newhaven, 10 miles north of Ashbourne. Unfortunately, as the aircraft was coming to a halt, it slewed round and crashed through a stone wall. This split open the wing fuel tanks, and the aircraft burst into flames and was completely burnt out. Tragically, three crew members, including the pilot, lost their lives. The wireless operator and rear gunner were the only survivors.

A third fatal accident, again this time at Hixon, occurred on Friday 10 September 1943 when a Wellington aircraft, visiting from RAF Lichfield, failed to gain sufficient height on take-off, also heading west from the main runway. So low was it that its starboard wing hit the corner of Wychdon Lodge (in New Road), damaging the house badly and losing part of its engine. The plane immediately crashed and skidded across the A 51 road before bursting into flames on the Western side of the road. Sadly, all five crew members were killed.

Wychdon Lodge on Station Road – this house was hit by a Wellington Aircraft on 10 September 1943

Not all accidents were the result of mistakes in training or equipment failure, however, and on a few occasions aircraft from Hixon were brought down by enemy action. The first of these recorded was on 14 April 1943 when seven Wellingtons from Hixon took off at 2115hrs to join eleven other planes on a 'nickel' raid over France. One of the Hixon planes was Wellington (DF610), piloted by F/Sgt Ball. The log book records that:

'Having completed his bombing run, F/S Ball was caught by searchlights as he turned away from the target and, despite his efforts to shake them off, the aircraft was hit both in the fuselage and then in the port engine. They finally escaped the searchlights but were losing height and it became clear that they would not make it back to England. Eventually they ditched the aircraft in the Channel, south of Dungeness at 0010hrs. Fortunately, all were safely rescued by the Air Sea Rescue Service.'

Not so fortunate were the crew of Wellington 'Z' (BK347). This plane is the one in the foreground in the well-known photo, used as a basis for the painting by Alan Preece which appears on the front cover of this book.

Vickers Wellington BK347, Hixon 'Z' which crashed in Yorkshire on 21 April 1944

This aircraft took off from Hixon during the afternoon of 21 April 1944 on a cross-country flight but, with dense cloud throughout the flight, the navigator probably struggled to establish their exact position. It is likely that they decided to descend below the cloud base to obtain a fix on their position but, unknown to the crew, they were many miles off-course, and over the high ground of Yorkshire. At 1615hrs, while probably still in cloud, the aircraft struck the moorland on the eastern side of Whernside, killing all the crew with the exception of the tail gunner, Sgt Marks.

The log book records other dramatic incidents which had a happier ending or even, as in this instance, a lucky escape. The report states that on 25 August 1943:

> 'Hixon's Wellington "O" (P/O Woodley) was struck by lightning whilst returning over Wales. The crew were preparing to bale out when the engine picked up again after seeming u/s so they carried on. On completing their detail over Bagot's Park, the starboard (front turret) gun suddenly fired a burst, so they returned to base at full speed. On examining the aircraft, it was found that there were large rents in the fuselage and that part of the propeller was missing.'

Another of the more dramatic training events, also thankfully without loss of life, was recalled in person a few years ago by Jim Syratt from Henley in Arden, then aged ninety-two years. He was a navigator and had started training with his new crew at Hixon in September 1943. By mid-November they had progressed to night-time training and, on Sunday 14 November, they were due to set off on a cross-country training flight. Jim explained that:

> 'We deemed the weather was unfit for flying as it was sleeting and snowing, and we were concerned the wings would ice up and the plane would not have the power to sustain flight. This decision was communicated to a senior officer – who was probably in the warm with a beer in his hands – but he was very dismissive and said we should go ahead and that if we didn't fly, we "would be off the course".

> 'This was the last thing we wanted so we set off. After about seventy-five minutes our fears were realised, and the plane started to lose height and become unstable. Our pilot ordered all the crew to bale out. The rear gunner went first, exiting his turret quickly. The rest of us followed and we all landed safely near Tenby in South Wales, though the aircraft crashed of course.'

Jim went on to say that he found a sheltered spot to lie in, wrapped in his parachute, while he collected his wits. Eventually he found a house and knocked on the door. The lady of the house who answered was distinctly unpleased to see him at that time of night and didn't make him at all welcome. He even had to ask if he could have a cup of tea.

Next morning the local police organised a taxi from the town to the station, then the crew, who had been reunited, had to make their way back to Hixon by train. Jim recalls that the pilot only had to fill in a short form explaining the loss of the plane, less than one side of paper!

It would appear that other crews also found the wintry conditions caused problems that night, with the station log book not only reporting the loss of Jim's plane, but showing that two others had narrow escapes:

0146hrs   *Hixon Wellington 'S' crashed near Tenby due to icing. Crew baled out.*

0216hrs   *Seighford's Wellington 'O' crash-landed at Jurby. No casualties.*

0245hrs   *Seighford's Wellington 'R' overshot at Llanwrog. No casualties.*

F/Sgt. Jim Syratt (then aged ninety-two) from Hampton in Arden holding his RAF log book

As a result of his experience Jim automatically qualified as a member of the 'Caterpillar Club' – that is for airmen whose lives have been saved by parachuting. On return to Hixon he went to the parachute room, a brick building somewhere near the parish church, and gave the person who had packed his parachute a gift of 2/6d as a thank you.

The names of the people who had used their parachutes were all written up on a board in the parachute room, together with the amount they had paid.

Jim's crew had several further 'hairy' experiences and crash landings, and after these the 'powers that be' decided, probably wisely, that the crew should be split up. Jim moved to fly with another crew, and they eventually flew sorties with three different squadrons, the final one being with 170 Squadron at Dunholm Lodge in Lincolnshire. From there he was posted as a navigation instructor to RAF Jurby in the Isle of Man, working there until the war ended in July 1945.

The 'Caterpillar Club' certificate in Jim Syratt's log book – this was awarded only to those whose lives had been saved by means of a parachute

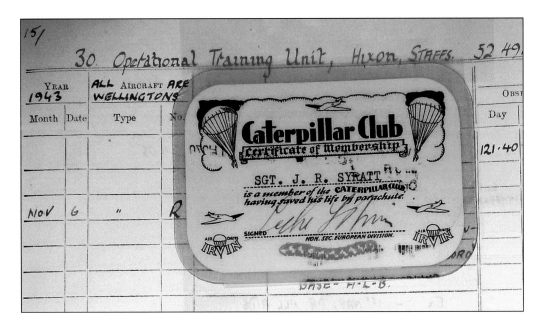

Flight Lieutenant Noel Burton from Rhodesia, already mentioned in Chapter Four, had returned to Hixon as a pilot instructor after completing and surviving his 'tour of ops'. It might be assumed that being based at a training OTU like RAF Hixon, rather than at a frontline RAF squadron, would be a safer option. This wasn't necessarily the case and Noel recalled two incidents which, he said, were every bit as frightening as operations against the enemy:

'On 11 August 1944 while instructing Flight Sergeant Player and crew on circuits and landings, the undercarriage would not fully lock down on our approach to land. We were therefore forced to overshoot the runway and climbed away for a further attempt to lock the undercarriage down, but the starboard engine started sounding rough and eventually had to be feathered.

'This prevented any delayed attempts to ensure that the undercarriage was locked down and we were forced to crash land. As there was no control of flaps, we landed at a higher speed than we would have liked and could not stop within the runway limits. The railway embankment was the ideal barricade to prevent us from going on and into the canal!

'Fortunately, this was, I believe, about thirty minutes before the main line train from Manchester was due at that point and the train was stopped by the signals before reaching the site. We all climbed out unscathed – another successful arrival!'

The second incident, just six weeks later, on 29 September 1944, was equally scary but fortunately was once again without injuries.

'Using Wellington "K" (BK297), on a test flight with F/Sgt. Williams and crew, prior to their taking the aircraft on a cross-country flight, we were over Cannock carrying out the usual aircraft check when a violent vibration went through the whole airframe.

'We soon realised that it was propeller damage to the starboard engine. Attempts to feather the blades proved impossible so we immediately set for home with the starboard engine cut, but we still suffered severe vibration as the airflow was rotating the damaged blades.

'Calling for a priority landing we did a single-engine approach with the fire tenders, ambulances, and emergency vehicles waiting their time for an immediate rescue operation.

'We landed safely and managed to clear the runway sufficiently to enable us to cut the port engine and come to a standstill, completely surrounded by the rescue crews who were looking a bit disappointed at the lack of further excitement, but exceedingly pleased to find us all happy and cheerful.

'A ground search at the Cannock Chase practice bombing range found a damaged propeller boss from a Wellington. It was translated into being the boss off the aircraft I had been flying. It had come off during flight and had damaged the feathering motor with the resultant inability to bring the engine to a halt. It was presumed that further severe vibration would have torn the engine loose from the mountings and inevitably led to a serious crash.'

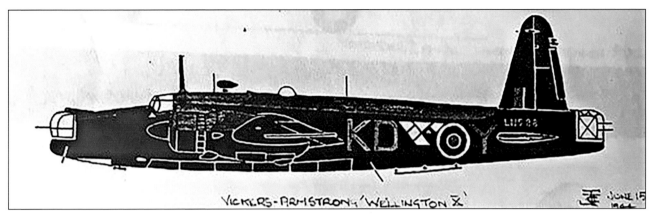

Hixon-based Wellington Mark X - KD-Y.
Picture drawn in 1944 by John Teasdale, then aged 14 years.

Over the three years when RAF Hixon was operating as No. 30 OTU, a total of fifty-three aircraft were lost in accidents. Not all were fatal of course. Four of these were lost on operations, probably all on 'nickel' runs, one was burnt out on the ground as detailed in Chapter Four, while the remaining forty-eight were lost on training flights of some description. (Further details can be found in Appendix 2.)

It is thus very evident that flying training at Hixon, and other operational training units, was a dangerous business, and accidents were not at all uncommon.

Nonetheless, despite the dangers and equipment failures, many hundreds of aircrew successfully completed their training at No. 30 OTU.

RAF Hixon can therefore rightly be said to have made a significant contribution to the success of the bombing campaign in Europe, something which in no small part led to the defeat of Germany and the liberation of Europe.

CHAPTER SIX

The End of the War and Closure of RAF Hixon – What Remains Today?

By the end of 1944 it was becoming clear that the war would probably soon be over. Indeed, serious consideration was already being given to possible post-war uses for the airbase. With this in mind, and with Air Ministry approval, the Lord Mayor of Stoke on Trent and two aldermen visited the airfield on Thursday 7 December 1944 to consider if it might be suitable for civilian use. In the event, whatever their decision, this never happened, and the airfield was retained by the RAF for several years after the end of the war.

In January 1945, possibly due to continued bad weather restricting flying time at Hixon, the operational decision was taken to move No. 30 OTU and all training activity to RAF Gamston in Nottinghamshire. Thus, almost overnight, all the Wellington aircraft left Hixon for the last time, together with very large numbers of personnel and ancillary equipment.

In their place, for the last few months of the war, No. 12 Pilots Advanced Flying Unit (PAFU) moved in, transferring from Spitalgate in Lincolnshire along with sixty Bristol Blenheim aircraft and, later, about thirty-five Bristol Beaufighters, plus various other different types of aircraft.

One of the ground crew who transferred from Spitalgate and who has shared her memories, was WAAF Wireless Operator Kate Perry (nee Porter) who worked in flying control based in the control tower. Her husband to be, mechanic Frank Perry, also transferred from Spitalgate. Both remembered Hixon as a happy place to be based with Cannock Chase nearby for walks on days off.

It was Kate who happened to be on duty at the teleprinter in the control tower on the night of 29 April 1945 and was very excited when at 0400hrs the following teleprinter message arrived. (The actual message says, with abbreviations and errors):

IS IT GEN THAT THE WARS OVER

YES AS FOR AS WE NO

WHO TOLD YOU

CAME OVER B/C (BBC)

TKS A LOT HAPPY V DAY

OH SURE THING

WE GOT OVER IT ON B/C LINE AND HEARD THAT THE PRDM HAD DENIED IT BUT HAVE SINCE GOT IT THAT IT IS QUITE TRUE

THANKS

Translated and in full the message reads:

> Is it true that the war's over?
>
> Yes as far as we know.
>
> Who told you?
>
> It came over on the BBC.
>
> Thanks a lot, Happy VE Day.
>
> Oh Sure thing! We got it on the BBC line and heard that the Prime Minister had denied it but have since found that it is quite true.
>
> Thanks

Recognising the importance and historic significance of this message, Kate sensibly kept and protected the printout and, sixty years later, kindly donated it to the author. It is reproduced below.

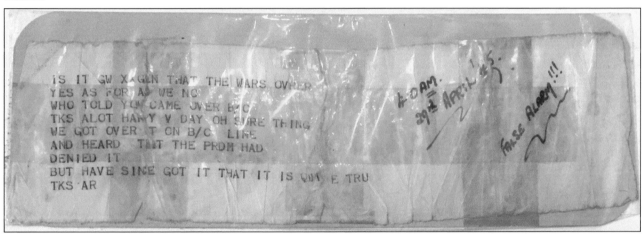

The original teleprinter message received at Hixon Control Tower on 29 April 1945

Thus it was that the war in Europe came to an end. All flying and training operations at RAF Hixon immediately finished, after what had been a hectic and dramatic three-year period of intense activity, effort and sacrifice.

Group Captain F E Rainsford, the last station commander of RAF Hixon, wrote the following moving and elegant testimony as the final entry in the station log book, summarising what had been achieved at No. 30 OTU, while also looking ahead to the work involved in building a peaceful future:

> **'Although this Unit has closed for the best of reasons – the end of the European War – its dissolution will be felt by many. The cheerfulness, enthusiasm and sterling work of all ranks achieved a spirit which will be an inspiration for the tasks of peace.'**
>
> **GROUP CAPTAIN F E RAINSFORD**

War surplus lorries lined up in storage on the former runways at RAF Hixon, after the War had finished.

Once flying and training at Hixon had ceased the airfield was handed over to the large equipment supply depot at 16 MU (Maintenance Unit) based nearby at Stafford.

They were in urgent need of storage space for the vast amount of war surplus equipment and before long the runways were full of hundreds of lorries and other vehicles parked, herring-bone fashion, the length of the runways. Gradually this equipment was sold or scrapped and eventually, in 1957, the airfield was reduced to a 'care and maintenance' basis. Five years later in 1962 it was sold for farming and light industrial use, a role it fulfils to this day.

What Remains Today?

Although it is more than seventy-five years since the airfield was in use, a number of buildings and structures remain in place, despite the fact that most of the buildings were intended to be temporary structures with an expected life span of only ten years.

The most obvious relics used to be the four very large and distinctive aircraft hangars, three on the main airfield site, the other on the south side of New Road. All four have, however been rebuilt in the last twenty years so are not so obvious.

Hangar 2 modified and in use by Agrii Ltd in 2021

Similarly, although two of the three original runways remain partly intact, these are no longer so easily seen as large sections are used for storage and distribution of second-hand cars for auction, and storage of damaged commercial vehicles and components. Other large sections of the original runways, and most of the perimeter tracks, have been dug up altogether.

These are, however, comparatively recent changes and for many years after closure the main runway was used by a private aircraft which was housed in a small hangar built at the railway end of the runway. Indeed, in May 1995, during the second Hixon History Society 'Wartime Years' Exhibition, this runway was used for no fewer than twenty-seven pleasure flights over the course of the May Bank Holiday weekend, giving a large number of people the opportunity, now lost, of flying from the wartime airbase.

The renovated original Control Tower with Fire-Engine Shelter to the left

Less easily seen perhaps, because it lies within the industrial estate complex, is the original Control Tower or, as originally designated by the RAF, the 'Watch Office'. This has been very well renovated and is used as offices by Hixon Airfield Services, which manages the industrial estate, and still has a splendid view across the whole airfield. Next to the Control Tower is a smaller building which was once a 'Fire Tender Shelter' housing a fire engine which could quickly be scrambled to the runways in the event of an emergency.

More easily visible to the public is the original 'Guard House' at the main entrance to the Industrial Estate on New Road. This has been renovated and is very well maintained by its

occupier, Central Fasteners Ltd. Next to this stands another small building, described on the original RAF plan as Building 41, 'Fire Tender House'. If one looks closely to the right-hand side of the entrance it is still possible to make out the original word 'FIRE' within a circle but now painted over.

Original Guard House in use by Central Fasteners Ltd at airfield entrance

Original Fire Engine House beside entrance Guard House 'FIRE' logo on right hand pillar

Further away on Egg Lane, and at a safe distance from the action on the outskirts of the village, stand the remains of the airbase hospital. These have long been used as farm buildings, together with the ruins of a couple of small guard houses nearby. Interestingly, immediately after the airbase closed, this and many of the other former accommodation buildings around the area, were taken over by people who could not afford houses of their own, or whose houses had been damaged in the war. The fascinating accompanying photograph, donated by Mrs Pelikan from Stafford, shows one such family moving in soon after the war, complete with children and their toys!

The remains of the RAF hospital in Egg Lane, together with a couple of guard houses behind

A delightful photograph of a family moving into a vacated wartime accommodation building
as a temporary home.

Although most such occupation was short lived, the former officers' mess, situated on the road out of the village beyond the school, remained in use as the main home of Mr and Mrs Bacon for several decades after the airbase closed. It has since been rebuilt and is now used as offices by Willow Senior Care Services.

Several of the RAF instructional and accommodation buildings in the same area are still in use as small industrial units and the nearby headquarters of Selwood Plant Hire occupy another former RAF building.

A further, rather more inventive use of a former RAF facility used to be situated beside the B1 Hangar on the left leaving the village. Here, the last remaining circular concrete dispersal bay was taken over by the police and for many years was used as a skidpan for training police drivers.

Former RAF buildings still in use by light industry

Large storage building with original shooting butts brick wall incorporated as central roof support

Although not an RAF building itself, Wychdon Lodge, on the left-hand side of New Road towards the A51, is also of significance. This is because, as described in Chapter Five, this substantial private house, which was spared from demolition before the war, was actually hit by an aircraft which tragically then crashed, killing all the crew

A less well-known or visible feature of the airfield which also still exists is a huge wall alongside the railway line. This wall, 3 feet thick and more than 20 feet high, was once the shooting butts where the guns of Wellington bombers were test fired. In front of the main wall and side walls were large piles of sand used to absorb the bullets fired at the wall. After the war the sand and side walls were removed, and the main wall was incorporated into a large barn as the central support for the roof. Once standing on its own alongside the railway, the barn has more recently been joined by several other large industrial buildings and connected with New Road by a new access road.

Thus, even today, with a keen eye it is not difficult to spot various buildings dotted around the district which remain as reminders of Hixon's wartime role and of the radical and permanent change which the construction and operation of RAF Hixon made to the village of Hixon and its community.

Internal view to show massive shooting butts wall

It is a history of which Hixon can be proud and it is appropriate and fitting that, in addition to the plaque in St Peter's Church commemorating the airmen who lost their lives while based at Hixon, there will soon be a stained-glass window reminding us of the amazing activity and sacrifice which took place in and around the village during the Second World War.

(Details of the new stained-glass window are given in Chapter Eight.)

Shooting Butts Barn

Scrap Vehicles on Runway

Control Tower

Truncated Main Runway

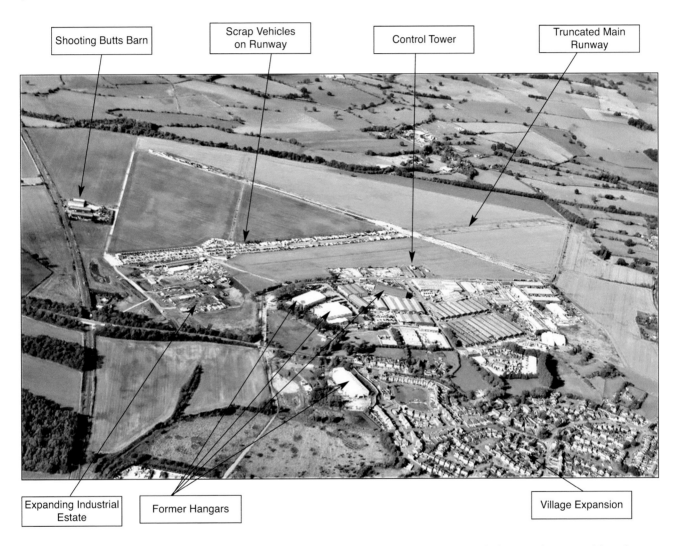

Expanding Industrial Estate

Former Hangars

Village Expansion

Aerial View of Hixon Airfield taken in October 2021 showing present conditions and changes that are taking place
(Compare with photo on Page 3)

CHAPTER SEVEN

Personal Stories of Two Brave Airmen

Every one of the airmen who arrived for training at RAF Hixon had already had many months of training and each would have had fascinating personal stories to tell. We are fortunate to have much more detail about two airmen, both from overseas; one whom was killed while training at Hixon; the other who survived the war and led a full and active family and professional life back in Tasmania.

1. The story of an airman who lost his life while in training at RAF Hixon

Sergeant Deryck Rowse from New Zealand

Sgt. Derek Rowse in Royal New Zealand Air Force (RNZAF) uniform

Sergeant Deryck Rowse is one of five overseas airmen buried in Hixon Churchyard and named on the memorial plaque inside St Peter's Church. He was killed, aged just thirty-one years, along with the other four members of his crew, at 1:15am on Tuesday 7 February 1943 when his Wellington aircraft crashed at nearby Ingestre Rectory after a failed attempt to land back at their RAF Hixon base.

Deryck Rowse was not from Britain but from New Zealand, the other side of the world. He lived on a dairy farm at Paraparaumu on the North Island of New Zealand, about 30 miles north of the capital city of Wellington. He had married Reina, a primary school teacher, in 1934 and they had two children, Judy, born in January 1936, and Roderick in November 1937.

He volunteered for the Royal New Zealand Airforce in 1941 to train as a wireless operator and in the full knowledge that, after initial training in NZ, his specialist training would be overseas followed by probable posting to the RAF in the UK.

Rowse family photo (1941)

His motivation for this dramatic decision, which meant leaving his wife and young family, will probably never be known. However, Andy Anderson, a specialist aviation historian who compiled a biography of Deryck for his family, said that while it might be that Deryck felt a burning desire to 'get at the enemy', it was just as likely that the war gave him an exciting opportunity to escape the hardships of life after the 1930s depression and to 'see a bit of the world'. Sadly, his decision meant that Deryck never saw his wife or two young children again, nor they their husband and father.

Deryck did indeed 'see a bit of the world'. After initial training in NZ his specialist training as a wireless operator was in Canada. He sailed there by ship, leaving on 22 September 1941, and made calls at Fiji, Samoa, Hawaii, Los Angeles and San Francisco en route to Vancouver. Once in Canada he started his training as a wireless operator at Calgary in October 1941 but unfortunately, after several months of training, he failed the course. He was felt to be better suited to a more practical task and accordingly was 're-mustered' to train as a rear gunner and moved to Fingal in Ontario for the course.

Derek's Crew at Hixon in January 1945, one month before the accident

Funeral cortege of Derek Rowse and Bob Lewis approaching St Peter's Church with airmen forming a guard of honour February 1945

This time he was successful and in August 1942 graduated as Sergeant Deryck Rowse, Air Gunner. While still in Canada and the USA he had periods of leave and had stays in both Montreal and New York before he was posted to Britain. He sailed from Halifax in Nova Scotia to Scotland, arriving safely in October 1942. From there he was quickly posted to No 30 Operational Training Unit at RAF Hixon to become part of a new crew and commence training.

Remarkably Deryck had relatives living not far away in Colton and visited them on more than one occasion. For his longest period of leave, however, he went to Cornwall, the county from where his Rowse family ancestors had emigrated to New Zealand. He really enjoyed this visit and, as his letters home reflected, 'found contentment and an affinity with Cornwall and its people'.

Back at RAF Hixon his crew would have followed the usual sequence of training activities detailed earlier in this book with ground training followed by a variety of daytime flying exercises, then similar exercises at night-time to prepare crews for night-time attacks on German or other enemy targets. As outlined in Chapter Two, one 'realistic' element of their training was to undertake lengthy cross-country flights of five to six hours duration within the UK, sometimes including bombing practice at ranges on Cannock Chase and elsewhere.

The headstone on the grave of Sergeant Derek Rowse, Air Gunner RNZAF, in St Peter's Churchyard, Hixon

Derek's crew had almost completed their training at RAF Hixon and, on Tuesday 7 February 1943, were returning from one of their final night-time cross-country flights. They had been in the air for 5 hours and 25 minutes when they attempted a landing at Hixon. For whatever reason Bob Lewis, the Australian pilot, decided to abort the landing and overshoot, and in the attempt to gain height the plane stalled and crashed by Ingestre Rectory, a couple of miles to the west.

The crew were all killed. In addition to Deryck as Rear Gunner, crew members included Bob Lewis (Pilot) from Australia and three men from the UK, namely Ken Austin (Navigator), Jock McGuiness (Air Bomber) and Joe Kenny (Wireless Operator).

Whereas the UK crew members would most likely have been buried in their home areas, Deryck and Bob were buried with full military honours at St Peter's Church in Hixon. The attached picture shows the funeral procession arriving at St Peter's Church with the coffins of Deryck Rowse and Bob Lewis on the back of a flatbed lorry acting as the hearse, and a close-up of Deryck's grave today.

Postscript: A Personal Perspective and Follow Up by Malcolm Garner

From the above it will be seen that, at the time of his death, Deryck's daughter Judy was just seven years old, and his son Roderick was just over five years old. Neither had seen their father for well over a year. Their memories of their father would therefore be fairly limited, and it was for this reason, and the fact that their mother didn't tell them much about their father after his death, that many years later Judy and Roderick commissioned an aviation historian (Andy Anderson) to undertake biographical research regarding their father's war service.

This resulted in a letter being sent to the vicar of Hixon in about 1997 to ask for information about the war memorial plaque in the church and Deryck's grave. Because of my own research into RAF Hixon, this letter was passed to me, and I was then able to make direct contact with Deryck's daughter, now married and called Judy Leader.

Judy was very pleased to have had this contact and sent a lovely message which was read out at the final Hixon History Society Meeting of the Millennium on Monday 6 December 1999. Judy said:

'During the war little was told to next of kin as to what actually happened to their loved ones and, as our mother died many years ago, we had little history, except for some photos of his grave in Hixon Churchyard which were sent at the end of the war by the British Ministry.

'It is through the Hixon History Society, and a friend here in New Zealand who has studied the histories of NZ airmen during the war, that my brother and I have been able to find out about the father we can hardly remember.

'I think it is wonderful that stories like ours stretch around the world and that, in a little way, we have a link with you and your village. I wish you an enjoyable evening and send you Christmas greetings.'

Malcolm with Judy Leader and son, Guy, at the crash site at Ingestre in 2002

Correspondence continued and it came as great surprise and pleasure when, one Saturday in 2002, I had a phone call out of the blue from Judy to say that she and her son Guy were in Stafford and would like to visit Hixon.

Fortunately, I was free that day so had the privilege of meeting them and showing them the airbase and local district plus, in a sombre and moving visit, showing Judy the site of her father's crash, close to Ingestre Rectory.

Fast forward the years to 2016 when I visited New Zealand myself, for the first time, on a cycling holiday. While there I took the opportunity, also unannounced, to drop in on Judy and her husband Bob at their home in Palmerston North. To my delight they were in good health and welcomed me warmly. Judy's younger brother Roderick lived nearby and in no time at all Judy called him, and he came across to meet me himself. Both were in good spirits and delighted to be reminded of their link to Hixon many thousands of miles away, yet so important in their own life story.

Later, during the same trip, I visited their childhood hometown of Paraparaumu, now a large and thriving suburb north of Wellington, and found the war memorial there which, like that at Hixon, also has the name of D C Rowse listed as a victim of World War Two.

I am sure Deryck would be astonished but also delighted to know that, more than seventy-five years after such a tragedy, there is still a personal link between people whose histories converge while they themselves live many thousands of miles apart.

Roderick and Judy (then a sprightly eighty year old!) with Malcolm at Judy's home in New Zealand in 2016

Malcolm Garner

2. The story of an overseas airman who survived the war

Pilot Officer Bill Gourlay from Australia

Bill Gourlay in Royal Australian Air Force (RAAF) uniform

Pilot officer Bill Gourlay was from Tasmania in Australia and was twenty-seven years old when he arrived at RAF Hixon. He was based here from July to September 1943 for initial crew training then, after completing and being fortunate to survive his 'tour of operations' (thirty flights over enemy territory), he returned to RAF Hixon from July 1944 to January 1945 as a navigation instructor before being repatriated back to Australia.

Before the war Bill worked in Launceston, Tasmania as a joiner and later an architectural draftsman and surveyor. In 1941 he heard the war in Europe was going badly and decided to volunteer his services. He was accepted into the Royal Australian Air Force Reserve (RAAF) and undertook a year of training in South Australia as an observer and navigator, flying in Avro Ansons, Hawker Demons and Fairey Battles.

In January 1943 he sailed from Melbourne to San Francisco aboard the *USS West Point* troop ship (converted from the nearly new luxury liner *SS America*) but then had to travel across America by train before joining another ship to get to Britain. This turned out to be none other than the famous passenger ship *Queen Elizabeth*, then in use as a troopship and carrying an amazing 17,000 service personnel on each voyage.

Further training in navigation followed before Bill was posted to No. 30 OTU at Hixon in July 1943 to 'crew up' and undertake the usual operational training course of day and night-time flying in a range of conditions. His pilot, Vic Neal, was also from Australia while other crew members were from Yorkshire, Durham and Wales.

Bill was a quiet and steady sort of guy and didn't always approve of the heavy drinking of some of the British crew members. Indeed, on one occasion two of them returned from a day's leave so drunk that they couldn't fly the next day and had to be replaced. They lost a week's leave as punishment.

'Australis' formerly USS 'West Point' **Troop Ship. Bill sailed from Melbourne to San Francisco aboard this ship in Jan 1943**

After completing their operational training in October 1943, the crew went to a heavy conversion course to learn to fly the larger Lancaster bombers, then joined 460 Squadron RAAF at Binbrook in Lincolnshire for their 'tour of operations'. Their first sortie was on 25 Feb 1944 when they bombed Augsburg in Germany. Bomber Command lost twenty planes on this raid and Bill's friend Reg Gill was among those posted 'missing'. Such losses inevitably had an effect on morale and Bill subsequently wrote in his diary:

'Before each trip one realizes two (often it is more) of our crews will not come back. No one says much but we think a lot, and everyone thinks it will be the other fellows. Official figures show that (only) one crew in four is finishing thirty trips OK. It is not that there Is a lot of risk on any one trip, but it is having to go thirty times that makes such odds.'

When one thinks of these odds, that 25 per cent of all Bomber Command crews would be shot down and killed or taken prisoner, the bravery of those continuing to fly and take on such dangers is inspiring and astonishing.

Although so many were lost, Bill's crew were one of those fortunate to have survived their 'tour of ops' and completed this in June 1944. After a well-earned period of leave they were then 'screened', that is removed from further active operations. As happened with a number of other aircrews after ops were completed, Bill was posted to an operational training unit as a navigation instructor whose task was to pass on his experience to trainee navigators. By chance or by design Bill found himself returning to 30 OTU at Hixon in July 1944 and was based there for the next six months.

Bill Gourlay's crew at RAF Blyton, Heavy Conversion Unit, Dec 1943
Bill Gourlay (Navigator) is second from right

The weather that winter was bitterly cold with 'frozen taps and frost on the ground for weeks'. Perhaps partly influenced by these conditions Bill and Vic Neal, the pilot from his crew and also an Australian, bravely volunteered for a second 'tour of ops'; this time on Mosquitos, which just had a two-man crew. They did initial training but then, out of the blue, Bill was informed that he should proceed to Brighton to begin arrangements for his repatriation home! This was a complete surprise but, as the war was obviously coming towards an end, it seemed sensible to accept this decision even though he had mixed feelings about it.

Thus it was that, on 22 April 1945, he boarded the Dutch Liner *Nieuw Amsterdam* at Gourock in Scotland. With an escort of two destroyers, they sailed south then through the Mediterranean and the Suez Canal en route to Australia. It was on 8 May, while on this voyage and in the Indian Ocean, that they heard about the victory in Europe. He was disappointed to be missing the celebrations going on in England and later wrote in his autobiography *Reward of the Years*:

'Today we have just had the grand news of final Victory in Europe, and in a few hours the ship will be crossing the Equator. What a great day for England! I wonder if there is one person aboard who does not wish that the ship could have sailed a fortnight later!'

Soon afterwards they reached Perth in Western Australia, then sailed on to Sydney and its spectacular harbour and bridge, a wonderful homecoming.

On arrival back home in Tasmania Bill wasted no time and became engaged to June two months later. They married in October 1946 with Vic Neal, his wartime pilot colleague and friend, as best man, then settled back into life in Tasmania. Bill qualified as an architect and enjoyed a successful thirty-six-year career with the City of Launceston Corporation in the city architect and building surveyor's department.

June and Bill had six children, four boys and two girls, and enjoyed a busy, active and happy family life in Launceston. They very much enjoyed sailing and, after several years with dinghies, built their own modest-sized yacht to sail and race. Bill also designed and built, latterly with considerable help from their children, each of their three houses. After Bill retired, he and June had the chance to visit the UK in 1985 as part of an extended international tour and met up with various friends and family relatives during their brief time here, though sadly they were not able to fit in a visit to Hixon.

Postscript: A Personal Perspective and Follow Up by Malcolm Garner

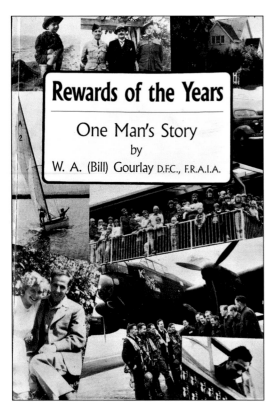

Bill's Autobiography 'Rewards of the Years', published in 1987

Bill had always kept in touch with the Jones family who, during the war, had very kindly offered him warm hospitality in their home at Shirleywich when he was based at Hixon. Their daughters Evelyn and Olive Jones, who were by the 1990s living at Rising Brook in Stafford, very kindly got in touch with me when the Hixon History Society were running their 'Wartime Years' Exhibitions in 1992 and 1995, to tell me about Bill. This enabled me to make contact with Bill in Tasmania and I enjoyed correspondence with him over several years.

In 1987 he had produced a well-written autobiography entitled *Reward of the Years* and he sent me a signed copy. It is full of fascinating detail regarding his life, and his wartime service in particular.

I, in turn, was able to send him one of the 'RAF Hixon' commemorative mugs we had produced for the History Society Exhibition in 1995 and he wrote to thank me for this, saying that it is a treasured memento and 'reposes behind glass in the wall cabinet'.

I learnt later that, sadly, Bill passed away in August 2002 at the age of eighty-six years. His daughter Robyn kindly sent me a copy of his original diary covering the wartime years and much of the above information has been assembled from his autobiography and these diary notes.

Bill was clearly a remarkable and, in many ways, a fortunate man. Unlike so many of his brave contemporaries and colleagues, he survived his time in action with RAF Bomber Command. He went on to live a very fulfilling and interesting life and was blessed with a happy marriage and a large family. I felt privileged to have been able to liaise with Bill, even though we never met, and to have learnt so much about his time in Hixon, where he was just one of the thousands of brave men and women who, through their commitment and sacrifice, helped win the Second World War. To have come half-way round the world to help do so seems even more remarkable.

Commemorative mug as sent to Bill Gourlay, produced by Hixon History Society in 1995

Reading Bill's delightful autobiography and learning about the very full and rewarding life he went on to lead after the war, only serves as a reminder of the many thousands of young men and women whose lives were cut short, and to be grateful for their sacrifice which helped preserve the way of life and freedoms we now enjoy.

Malcolm Garner

CHAPTER EIGHT

Hixon Commemorates the Wartime Years – 1992–1995–2022

In the 1990s the fiftieth anniversaries of wartime events came round, and the people of Hixon made special efforts to commemorate and celebrate the part that the village of Hixon, and RAF Hixon in particular, had played in the war effort.

1992

In 1992 we celebrated the fiftieth anniversary of the opening of the airbase. The recently formed Hixon Local History Society led the way with a three-day exhibition over the May Bank Holiday weekend held, appropriately, in the Hixon Memorial Hall.

Crowds waiting outside Hixon Memorial Hall for the Spitfire Flypast at the 'Wartime Years' Exhibition in May 1992

Unveiling of Commemorative Plaque in Hixon Memorial Hall by Officer Commanding No 16 MU, RAF Stafford, Saturday 2nd May 1992

An impressive collection of wartime artefacts and memorabilia was assembled, some lent by individuals, others by the Staffordshire Museums Service. These included such things as an airman's shirt button which was really a miniature compass to assist if he was shot down, and an original flight map from a bombing raid over enemy territory. There were also the more familiar and local ration books, Women's Land Army cap badges, gas masks, uniforms, wartime leaflets and various other smaller items of wartime memorabilia.

Several vintage vehicles were on display including a genuine 1942 RAF fire tender owned by Rob Brittlebank from Stafford.

At 3.00 pm on the Saturday afternoon a brass plaque, commemorating the many airmen who lost their lives in training while based at Hixon, was unveiled inside the Memorial Hall by the Officer Commanding RAF No. 16MU Stafford.

This was followed by what, for many, was the highlight of the weekend. This was a specially arranged flypast by a genuine 1943 Spitfire Mark IX, piloted by its then owner, businessman David Pennell.

It was arranged that he would fly over at 3.30 pm, by which time those involved in the plaque unveiling would be outside to see the flypast. There was a tense couple of minutes wondering if this would take place as the weather conditions had to be just right, but then with no warning because it came in so low, the Spitfire simply burst into view over the hall, with the wonderful sound of its Rolls Royce Merlin engine, and

1943 Mark IX Spitfire MJ730 at Hixon May 1992

roared over the crowd and climbed high over the village. It then swung back and swooped low two or three times over the hundreds of people who had gathered to watch it, before waggling its wings and flying away. It was a magnificent display and one that left everyone exhilarated.

Later that afternoon, unannounced, David Pennell drove to the hall and presented two items to add to the exhibits already at the hall. These were a damaged propeller blade from his Spitfire and also the original 1943 nose cone from the propeller. Such a kind gesture.

Spitfire MJ730 performing a low-level flypast at Hixon 'Wartime Years' Exhibition in May 1992

Several thousand people passed through the exhibition over the course of the three days, and it generated considerable publicity and additional interest in what had taken place on our doorstep all those years before.

1995

Three years later, in May 1995, an even more impressive follow-up exhibition was arranged. As well as a repeat of the indoor exhibition, though with many new exhibits, a range of other activities took place with other village groups taking an active part.

Carnival Float with pupils and staff from St Peter's Primary School (May 1995)

St Peter's Primary School, for example, entered a 'wartime years' float in the village Carnival with pupils wearing clothing of the 1940s and carrying gas masks in boxes. For their part, patrons of the Bank House Pub across the road erected a lifting barrier across the car park entrance and posted guards in uniform to 'challenge' anyone wishing to enter!

'Wartime checkpoint' with guards at Bank House Public House

The hall itself was surrounded by protective sandbags and all the windows had masking tape applied in the shape of a diagonal cross as had happened in wartime as protection in case of bomb blast.

Although there was no repeat of the Spitfire flypast a friend of the organiser brought his light aircraft to the airfield and, over the weekend, flew no less than twenty-seven pleasure flights, giving three passengers a time the unique opportunity to fly from the same main runway as used in wartime.

Another friend of the organiser brought his ex-Devon General double decker open-top bus and gave tours of the airfield, starting at the Memorial Hall each time and taking in the various remaining buildings such as the hangars and control tower. Dozens of people took the tour, and it was a real pleasure to see several men and women, who had served at RAF Hixon in the war, return for the weekend and thoroughly enjoy revisiting places they remembered so well from half a century before.

Hixon History Society 1995 Exhibition Organising Committee outside Hixon Memorial Hall with protective taped windows and sandbags

A commemorative mug was produced and 500 of these were sold over the weekend!

More important still, agreement was given for an additional memorial stone to be added to those already inset in the front wall of the memorial hall. This stone simply read:

VE Day – VJ Day 50th Anniversary 1945 – 1995

Local residents and wartime veterans enjoying an
open-top bus ride around the sights at RAF Hixon

Flight Lieutenant Steve Boylan and Mrs Boylan after
unveiling the memorial plaque

Local residents enjoying a 1940s dance with a Glenn Miller tribute band
during the fiftieth anniversary commemorations

We were greatly honoured that this was unveiled by none other than Flt Lt Steve Boylan who had served as a pilot instructor at the RAF base from 1942 – 1944 (see Chapter Four) and came from his home in Leek with his wife to perform the ceremony.

On the social side of the weekend a 1940s style dance was held in the Memorial Hall in the evening with a Glenn Miller Tribute band. Everyone was dressed either in uniform or in clothing of the wartime era and an enjoyable time was had by all!

Mr and Mrs Rob Brittlebank and family in period costume with their
1942 RAF Fire Tender

Several military vehicles attended the event on each day. These included an original RAF Fuel Bowser Lorry (as depicted in the front cover painting) which came from Leicester and, once again, the 1942 RAF Fire Tender driven by its owner, Rob Brittlebank from Stafford who came complete with his own family in period clothing.

Finally, on the earth bank on the opposite side of the road from the Memorial Hall, two large letters were carved and filled with chalk dust, rather like the White Horses carved into some of the chalk downlands in the south of England. The two letters were V E. This obviously really referred to 'Victory in Europe', but one wag suggested that we had intended to write VERA LYNN but simply ran out of room!

So, as can be seen from just this brief description, the villagers of Hixon not only had a thoroughly enjoyable weekend, but also did their best to provide an appropriate commemoration of the dramatic events that had taken place in their village fifty years earlier.

Large VE letters carved into the bank opposite the Hixon Memorial Hall in celebration and commemoration of victory in Europe, fifty years before

Commemorative mug produced by Hixon
Local History Society for the 50th
nniversary of VE Day in 1995

2022

In more recent years there has been renewed interest in various aspects of the history of the village of Hixon including, among other things, the 1968 Railway Level Crossing Disaster and also the wartime RAF base in the village.

As part of this increased focus, the railway industry generously contributed funds to maintain the commemorative garden established at St Peter's Church in 1968 to remember the fiftieth anniversary of that accident. In addition, these funds have generously made possible the installation of two new stained-glass windows in St Peter's Church, one to commemorate each of these very significant features of Hixon village history.

The rail disaster will be represented by an image of the famous British Rail Lion and Wheel emblem. In the case of the RAF however, in the absence of a station specific RAF badge for RAF Hixon, the image will be of a roundel as carried by RAF aircraft. This window is already completed and will be installed in the near future, once appropriate agreements have been obtained.

This window will then, in addition to the existing wooden plaque with names of those airmen buried in the churchyard, form a permanent reminder of the very significant part Hixon played in the Second World War and the sacrifice of very many brave men and women during that conflict.

Stained Glass Window to commemorate
RAF Hixon, ready to be installed in St
Peter's Church in 2022

Chronology of No. 30 OTU

R.A.F. HIXON ~ 1941 – 1962

Based closely on records in the original Station Log Book, now lodged with the
Public Record Office at Kew

25 September 1941

Local Defence Adviser Major A Nichol arrived on site to locate defence posts. These were the points arounds the area where defence teams would be deployed in the event of an attack on the airbase.

13 May 1942

The first airmen were posted to Hixon from No. 27 OTU, RAF Lichfield, which initially acted as the parent station. They were initially accommodated on No. 9 site.

22 May 1942

The Institute commenced to function.

25 May 1942

Flight Lieutenant J L Girling assumed command.

28 June 1942

No. 30 Operational Training Unit (OTU) was officially formed for night bomber training.

June & July 1942

Personnel were arriving at the base throughout these months. The WAAF section was formed on 2 July.

15 July 1942

The first two aircraft arrived at Hixon at 1230hrs. They were Vickers Wellington Mk.1C medium bombers from No. 12 OTU at Chipping Warden and were not flown again, being used as instructional airframes at the base. The runways were not fully completed and they used improvised smoke indicators and green Very lights to help with the landing.

17 July 1942

Air Vice Marshal Capel, Air Officer Training, visited to discuss training.

19 July 1942

First Church Parade (C of E and OD) held in station church – 250 attended. Service led by Rev W H Dodd, Vicar of Weston.

23 July 1942

The first three operational Wellingtons arrive. Eventually there were to be thirty attached to the airbase.

29/30 July 1942

One further Wellington arrives each day making a total of seven, two of which were partially dismantled and placed in the instructional fuselage building.

8 August 1942

The first course of aircrew training commenced with twenty-nine pupils.

23 August 1942

The second course commenced with thirty pupils and the first course started flying. A concert by was given by the Black Velvet Company.

27 August 1942

Concert by No. 16 MU Band.

Cinema shows commenced twice weekly by Army Film Unit.

Defence posts were established around the area and ten fighting patrols were formed. These were in sectors and bases included Stowe Railway Station, the White Barn and the Sick Quarters on Egg Lane.

3 September 1942

Number three course started.

September 1942

Entertainments were getting well under way. Hixon Concert Party (with Wilmot Martin) gave shows at the base on 9/10/11 September and at 16 MU on 16 September. Dances were held in the corporals' club every Tuesday and another concert was held on the 20th and Cello Recital on 30th.

13/14 September 1942

The first operational sortie. Three Wellington aircraft (DV771/T2475/X9801) took off at 2340hrs and joined 475 other aircraft to attack the German industrial City of Bremen. Two of the Hixon aircraft arrived over the target, the other failed to find it as the compass was u/s. X9801 was shot up on the return, west of Einkhuisen. Overall the raid was a success and all three aircraft returned safely.

16/17 September 1942

Four Wellingtons (DV448/T2475/DV613/DV771) took off between 1922 and 1937hrs to join 365 other aircraft over the North Sea to attack the city of Essen. However, one aircraft (DV613) returned to base with its bomb load due to faulty manipulation of bomb switches. Another (DV448) had intercom trouble and difficulty in climbing so that it could not gain sufficient height and had to turn back. The other two reached the target and were able successfully to bomb the city.

16 September 1942

Number one course commenced night training.

13 October 1942

The Hixon Station Party gave its first concert.

24 October 1942

Number one course went out.

24 October 1942

Wellington 1C (DY952) piloted by Sgt Burton took off at 2107hrs on 'nickel' raid over France. Successfully dropped 700lb nickel. Slight flak and searchlight opposition but arrived back safely at 0140hrs.

October/November 1942

Entertainment Committee was established and strengthened. Cinema shows now held every Tuesday, Wednesday and Thursday. Also various dances and concerts. Coaches, holding thirty-six airmen each, run under the auspices of the Workers Travel Association to munitions hostels at Swinnerton.

2 November 1942

New indoor rifle range opened with evening practice using .22 rifles.

6 November 1942

Station Band played at a dance at Stowe by Chartley.

7/8, 11/12, and 22/23 November 1942

'Bullseye' exercises.

NOTE: A 'bullseye' exercise was a navigation exercise to a simulated target in the UK, usually one of the larger cities (sometimes from Hixon the King George V Dock in London). The target was indicated in many cases by an upward shining infra-red light and crews were expected to return with a 'bombing photo' of the target.

4/5 December 1942

Hixon Concert Party again in action at the base.

December 1942

Small outbreak of mumps. Four officers and eighty-seven other ranks were admitted to the sick bay during December. Also this month Sgt Drayton, Air Gunner, died of shock, burns and a broken left leg following a flying accident. No other details of the cause of this are given.

December 1942/January 1943

Following the disbandment of 25 OTU, the size of 30 OTU at Hixon was increased by the transfer of twenty-six Wellingtons and their crews from RAF Finningley. The first additional aircraft, a Mk III Wellington, arrived on 28 December.

3 January 1943

The Bishop of Lichfield dedicated the station church. There was a full parade of airmen and women and a large number of officers.

15 January 1943

Hixon Concert Party again.

14/15 January 1943

Further 'nickel' raids (to Rouen).

29/30 January 1943

'Bullseye' exercise with nine aircraft. Three returned to Hixon, six went elsewhere.

February 1943

The unit's strength stood at fifty Vicker's Wellington medium bombers. Thirty-five were Mark III and fifteen were Mark X. Most Mark 1C Wellingtons had left and the six remaining were allocated and were to be despatched after overhaul.

Large numbers of personnel were billeted in and around the airbase. At maximum the figures were:

	Officers	S.N.C.O.'s	Other Ranks	Total
RAF	204	510	1,679	2,393
WAAF		10	435	445
			Total Personnel	2,838

February 1943

Several 'nickel' raids dropping leaflets over Paris:

13/14 – Three Wellingtons.

15/16 – Two Wellingtons.

25/26 – Seven Wellingtons.

March 1943

RAF Hixon provided a guard of honour for a fighter aircraft which was displayed on Milford Common as part of 'Wings for Victory' week. £115,000 was raised by the people of Stafford and District.

Further 'nickel' raids on 4th (five planes) and 23rd (four planes).

23/25 March

Hixon Concert Party performed at the base and at Seighford on the 30th .

April 1943

Aircraft from Hixon had completed twenty-three sorties on 'nickel' operations. These were missions to drop propaganda leaflets, rather than bombs, and were a useful training experience.

14 April 1943

The first plane was lost as a result of enemy action. This was Wellington DF610, one of seven such planes from Hixon in a force of eighteen undertaking a 'nickel' raid over France. Having completed his bombing run, F/S Ball was caught by searchlights as he turned away from the target and, despite his efforts to shake them off, the aircraft was hit both in the fuselage and then in the port engine. They finally escaped the searchlights but were losing height and it became clear that they would not make it back to England. Eventually they ditched the aircraft in the Channel, south of Dungeness. Fortunately all were safely rescued by the Air Sea Rescue Service.

16/17 & 26/27 April 1943

Further 'nickel' raids with six and four aircraft respectively

April 1943

In addition to the film shows three times/week, there were now dances every Wednesday and Sunday. Also the Workers Travel Association ran buses from Hixon to hostels at Frobisher and Swinnerton three times/week to the dances.

May 1943

'Nickel' raid on the 4th with six Wellingtons. One of these crash-landed at Greenham Common on return. Further 'nickel' raids on 23rd (two Wellingtons), 24th (two), 27th (two) and 30th (three).

May 1943

The cinema was rebuilt with two new 35mm projectors, opening on the 17th. Fitted with 'tip-up' seats. Film shows six nights/week with the programme changed every Monday and Thursday. Dances were held regularly and every Sunday.
Two lectures during the month, one on 'art', the other on 'Zionism'.

3/4 June 1943

Seven Wellingtons carried out a 'nickel' raid over France (Paris three, Lorent two, Brest two). A total of 137 packages were dropped.

11/12 June 1943

Three Wellingtons dropped forty-two packages over Nantes. One aircraft (Wellington 'K' F/Sgt. Dellar) failed to return.

22/23 June 1943

Sixteen aircraft were despatched to take part in four 'nickel' raids over France (Paris, Orleans, Le Mans and Rheims). One returned early due to technical failure, while another landed at West Malling following a fire in the starboard engine off Beachy Head. Sadly, another Wellington X (HE527), piloted by F/S Hennessy failed to return and the crew were all posted as missing, presumed killed in action. The remaining aircraft dropped 227 packages.
(In fact three of the crew of HE527 parachuted to safety over Cherbourg where they were caught and sent to prison camps for the duration.)

1943

During this year some Curtiss Tomahawk fighter aircraft were attached to the OTU at Hixon. They were joined later by Masters, Martinets and Hurricanes. These were used to undertake mock attacks on the Wellingtons as training exercises (fighter affiliation).

1/2 July 1943

Further 'nickel' raid with eight Wellingtons. One ('C' BK255 Capt.Sgt.Fisher) crashed at Exeter on return and burnt out, killing all but the rear gunner. Other seven aircraft arrived back safely.

6/7 July 1943

'Bullseye' training exercise with six aircraft. One crashed near the 'Wicket' Inn killing all on board.

9/10 & 13/14 July 1943

Further 'bullseye' exercises with seven aircraft on each occasion

12/13 July 1943

'Nickel' raid with six Wellingtons. All returned.

24 July 1943

The United States Deputy Assistant Chief of Staff, Brigadier General Bennett-Meyers arrived at 1930hrs to carry out an inspection of the unit's training methods. He was accompanied by his ADC, Wing Commander Beckwith and F/O Wyatt from the Air Ministry. He stayed overnight and inspected an armed guard of honour. The log records that 'he seemed very interested and took notes'. He left at 1200hrs next day for High Ercall.

August 1943

Several further 'nickel' and 'bullseye' exercises.

30/31 August & 1 September 1943

Aircraft flew three sorties over Northern France attacking ammunition dumps at Fort D'Eperlecques. A total of forty 500lb bombs and one 4,000lb bomb were successfully dropped on target. Aircraft involved were BK146, X3565, HE407, HE505, HE 503, BK358, BJ988, X3353.

September 1943

'Bullseye' and 'Nickel' operations on seven occasions.

8 September 1943

Three aircraft attacked Boulogne. Two successfully dropped sixteen 500lb bombs, the other aborted. Aircraft were X3939, X3883, BJ986.

29 September 1943

There were several visits by senior RAF officers to view the unit. These included Sir Edgar R Ludlow Hewitt KGB CMG DSO MC, Inspector General of the RAF.

30 September 1943

Geoffrey Manders MP, Personal Private Secretary to the Secretary of State, visited.

September 1943

Progress reported on the link trainer and GROPE exercises (ground operations).

1 October 1943

Piano recital by F/L Glock.

2 October 1943

RAF gang show and ENSA (Entertainments National Service Association) play.

6 November 1943

The first night-navigation exercises using homing radio operation.

29 November 1943

Twelve American and South African pilots and navigators visited the UK and Hixon to obtain knowledge of bad weather flying!

December 1943

The first recorded diversion of aircraft from other bases. Five Stirlings from Leicester East all landed safely between 2200hrs and 2300hrs after a raid on German flying bomb sites.

January 1944

The Air Ministry made an official history of bomber training and used four Wellingtons from Hixon. Two were detailed to drop bombs on ranges at Rufford and Ragdale while two others carried the press photographers. Reports apparently appeared in the national press.

13 January 1944

Hixon supplied six aircraft to assist in air-sea search over North Sea. Nothing found.

24 March 1944

Air raid warning at 0112hrs. All clear at 0145hrs.

27 February 1944

Snow! The snow plan was put into operation and the airfield was useable again by 1100hrs on twenty-eighth.

April 1944

Four Martinet aircraft were replaced by Hawker Hurricanes.

5 May 1944

Visit to 16MU, Stafford by Sir Archibald Sinclair. A secret cypher message had been received on 3 May 1944 from HQ Transport Command.

'Secretary of State for Air, Sir Archibald Sinclair leaving HENDON passenger 0900hrs 5 May, in 24 Squdn. Flamingo arriving HIXON 0945hrs. leaving HIXON by car for No.16 MU Stafford, arriving 1015hrs. leaving at 1045hrs. for HIXON. Maintenance Cmd. requested to provide car to No 16 M.U. and back to HIXON. Leaving HIXON by air 1200hrs. for BALLYKELLY arriving 1330. Ballykelly requested to provide lunch. Leaving Ballykelly 1500hrs. for Wick arriving 1730hrs. Leaving Wick p.m. for Castledown. Castltown requested to provide car to Thurso castle. Leaving Castletown 1000hrs. for Coningsby arriving 1215hrs. Coningsby requested to provide lunch. Leaving Coningsby 1430hrs for Hendon.'

June 1944

An emergency air bottle for lowering the undercarriage of Wellington aircraft was introduced throughout Bomber Command. It was originally designed at 30 OTU Hixon and subsequently received the approval of Bomber Command Headquarters.

30 June 1944

American General George S Patton Junior flew in to inspect a prisoner of war camp in Rugeley. More regular American visitors were en route to the Combat Crew Replacement Centre at Stone. On one occasion no less than twenty-three Douglas C-47 aircraft flew in although more often the American aircraft were B-17s and B-26s.

31 July 1944

Six Lancasters were diverted from Kelstern.

6 August 1944

Ten Halifaxes diverted from Sandtoft and one from Lindholme.

1 October 1944

First 'Annual Field Day' held for Midland Command Air Training Corps and affiliated squadrons. Great success. Competitions in navigation, signals, airmanship, aircraft recognition and shooting.

28 October 1944

The satellite base at Seighford was transferred to Flying Training Command.

20 November 1944 – 1144hrs

Wellington (LP544) caught fire in hangar. No cause apparent. Aircraft u/s. *(See Chapter Four for details. Discrepancy in aircraft number and time as recorded in different documents.)*

7 December 1944

As arranged by Air Ministry, the Lord Mayor of Stoke on Trent and two aldermen visited RAF Hixon for the purpose of inspecting the aerodrome as to its suitability for civil aviation after the war.

2 February 1945

No 30 OTU moved complete from Hixon to a new base at Gamston. All forty-one Wellingtons flew to their new base, quite a change for Hixon after several years of round-the-clock flying by the bombers. Moving at the same time were 167 officers, 992 other ranks, 4 WAAF officers and 314 WAAF other ranks. Flying started at Gamston on 4 February. The OTU continued training at Gamston until it was finally disbanded on 12 June 1945.

3 February 1945

No. 12 Pilots Advanced Flying Unit (PAFU) moved to Hixon from Grantham. In place of the Wellingtons came sixty-two Blenheims, thirty-six Oxfords and three Beauforts.

May 1945

The Blenheims were gradually replaced by Beauforts and the last four flew to Filton in Bristol for breaking up.

21 June 1945

No. 12 PAFU was disbanded and the remaining thirty-eight Beauforts were flown to No. 44 MU. RAF Hixon now became a sub-site of No. 16 Maintenance Unit at Stafford.

1946/47/48

The airfield was used as a collecting point and store for redundant military vehicles. At one time all the runways were lined from end to end with vehicles parked in 'herring-bone' fashion. They were gradually sold for further use or scrap and driven away.

5 November 1957

The airfield was reduced to inactive status.

1962

The airfield was sold by the Ministry of Defence for industrial and agricultural purposes.

Details of Accidents and Incidents as Recorded in the Original Station Log Book

Supplemented by information from a variety of other sources

NO. 30 OTU – RAF HIXON

11 September 1942

Wellington (N2779), piloted by Sgt Stitt, came in too fast while doing circuits and bumps (landings), overshot across the Euston to Manchester railway line. The aircraft was only slightly damaged and the only casualty, Air Gunner Sgt Bateman, sustained only minor cuts and slight shock.

22 September 1942

Wellington (DV486), Pilot Sgt Smitheringdale, doing circuits and bumps made a heavy landing distorting tail wheel frame.

1 October 1942

Wellington 1C (Z8968) swung off the runway when landing. The pilot over corrected and the aircraft skidded. When the tyres gripped the undercarriage collapsed through side-stress. The crew of four were OK except for Sgt E T Bakeman, who was injured.

9 October 1942

The operational records book records that a Boulton Paul Defiant 1, piloted by P/O Bartley, collided with a horse and cart while taxying. The record states that 'the horse appeared bruised and damage was caused to the leading edge of the starboard mainplane and one of the airscrew blades'.

31 October 1942

An accident occurred which brought the unit's first fatalities. Wellington IC (Z1083) was practising circuits with F/S Belgrove as the pilot and W/O Primrose as the instructor. At 2050hrs the plane stalled at 500ft and crashed and burst into flames at Grange Farm, Amerton, adjacent to the northern boundary of the airfield. The crew of six were all killed. They were F/S Belgrove, W/O Primrose, P/O Hegan (Navigator), F/S Cunningham (Wireless Operator), F/S Hawk (Air Gunner) and F/S Woolliams

(The latter two, both Canadians, are buried in St Peter's Churchyard, Hixon).

28 November 1942

Following engine failure on take-off, Wellington I X9801 crashed into some trees, probably on the north side of the A518 near Weston Bank.

19 December 1942

Wellington 1C (DV952). Engine backfired and cut out completely when approaching the Isle of Man on a navigational exercise. After a check they were able to land safely at Jurby.

9 January 1943

Wellington 1C (X.9825). While returning from a cross-country flight, the undercarriage collapsed on landing owing to aircraft swinging to avoid running into dispersed aircraft. The pilot was overshooting due to difficult conditions and on attempting to go round again he opened the throttle too quickly and the engine backfired. He then put the airscrew into coarse pitch thinking this would increase drag but it had the adverse effect.

13 January 1943

Wellington 1A (P2532). Smoke appeared in the aircraft. The undercarriage refused to come down when an emergency landing was attempted at Tatenhill. A successful crash landing was made at Hixon.

22 January 1943

Wellington 1C (Z8847). The port tyre burst on landing and the aircraft tipped up on its nose causing damage to both airscrews, tail wheel and the nose of the aircraft.

25 January 1943

Wellington Mk3 (DF641). When on a cross-country flight the aircraft hit the top of a tree at the end of the take-off run due to failure in the constant speed unit on the port engine. The airscrew thereby remained in fully fine pitch, giving excessive slip.

2 February 1943

An airman was slightly injured when he walked into the propeller of Vickers Wellington X (HE428). The entry in the records states only that 'The propeller was badly damaged'.

3 February 1943

Wellington III (BK184) made a crash landing at Skerry Hall Farm, near Thorpe, Robin Hoods Bay when on a navigation exercise flight. Starboard engine caught fire in mid-air and pilot couldn't maintain height. Both crew survived. No blame was attached to the pilot Sgt J King. The navigator Sgt Payne was injured in the crash.

7 February 1943 – 1000hrs *(crash happened at 0115hrs)*

Vickers Wellington III (BK434) stalled at 1000ft and crashed into Horseshoe Covert at Ingestre Hall on the Ingestre Estate. The crew of five were all killed. These included Pilot R D Lewis (Australian) and Air Gunner D C Rowse (New Zealander). Both these airmen are buried in St Peters Churchyard, Hixon. *(See Chapter Seven for biography of Deryck Rowse.)*

7 February 1943

Wellington III (X3332) overshot at Seighford. No injuries. Pilot coming in too fast.

10 February 1943

A Miles Master aircraft from No. 3 Pilots Advanced Flying Unit crashed near the airfield, fortunately without casualties.

13 February 1943

Wellington X (HE466) crashed near Snowdon (Foel Grach O/S 115 Ref: 692664). Pilot F/S E G Frezell. All crew killed. Flew into mountain in cloud.

16 February 1943

Wellington III (BK251) made a heavy landing at Westcott. Undercarriage damaged. The starboard engine failed and the pilot had to do his best on one engine. On landing the aircraft swung off the runway causing the port undercarriage to collapse.

10 April 1943 (or 10 January)

Wellington III (BK159) appeared to stall soon after take-off at night. The aircraft crashed and all the crew were killed.

10 April 1943 0530hrs

The pilot, navigator and air bomber of Wellington III (DF611) were killed when the aircraft crashed at Hartington, Derbyshire.

The aircraft was on a night-time bomb aiming practice when, twenty-five minutes into the flight, one engine failed and the other one started running rough. The pilot decided to attempt an emergency landing. He managed to do a 'wheels-up' landing on the main road (which was particularly straight at this point) but unfortunately as the aircraft was coming to a halt, it slewed round and crashed through a stone wall. This spilt open the wing fuel tanks and the aircraft went up in flames and was completely burnt out.

Crew:	Pilot	F/Sgt R A Jones	Killed
	Navigator	F/Sgt J F Spencer	Killed
	Bomb aimer	F/Sgt G K Parsons	Killed
	Wireless operator	F/Sgt R J Perrin	Survived
	Rear gunner	F/Sgt J Douglas	Survived

(Many thanks to Marshall Boylan for these details.)

11 April 1943

Wellington III (DF640) was damaged when a tyre burst on landing.

14 April 1943

The first plane was lost as a result of enemy action. This was Wellington III DF610, one of the seven such planes which took off from Hixon at 2115hrs in a force of eighteen undertaking a 'nickel' raid over France. *(See Appendix 1 for full details.)*

22 April 1943

Wellington III (DF641). The pilot did not put the propellor into fine pitch on coming into land and made a belly landing to the left of the runway.

23 April 1943

Wellington X (HE390) taxied into Lysander N1308 which was at the end of a runway. The port wing leading edge was buckled, port propeller smashed and port exhaust ring of the Wellington was buckled. The Lysander was badly damaged.

29 April 1943

Wellington III (X3564) was passing a lorry which was on the LH side of the perimeter track at Sealand when they collided. The log states that 'the lorry suddenly moved forward and collided with the mainplane of the aircraft'.

30 April 1943

The starboard engine of Wellington III DF618 cut on take-off and the aircraft was damaged.

5 May 1943 – 0215hrs

Wellington III (BJ970). Crash-landed at Greenham Common. The lower surface of the fuselage smashed, undercarriage was wrecked, port mainplane damaged and engines shock loaded.

12 May 1943

Wellington III (BK363). Accident at Sealand (crash landing).

15 May 1943 – 0357hrs

A Wellington III (HE468) on a non-operational night training flight stalled and crashed at Mountford Farm, Salt Heath. All the crew were killed. They were:

Pilot:	Flt. Officer J H G Watson
Navigator	Sgt G A Cure
W.Op. air gunner	Sgt T J Campbell
Bomb aimer	P/O E G Farrow
Air gunner	Sgt D P Boyle
Air gunner	Sgt J Hedge

Also killed was an army officer (Lt P A Roberts) who was a passenger.

(Thanks to Chris Howard from Norfolk for additional information.)

15 May 1943

Wellington III (BK139). Accident at Llandwrog. Aircraft was burnt and was a write-off.

22 May 1943

Wellington (BJ618). Accident at Hixon. Damaged port mainplane, nacelle and side of rear fuselage. Engine shock loaded. Category AC *(i.e., repairable but beyond the unit's capacity)*.

22 May 1943

Wellington III (DF546). Accident at Seighford.

23 May 1943

Wellington (BK251). Accident at Seighford.

30 May 1943

Wellington III (BK443). Accident at Hixon. Starboard mainplane, port and starboard nacelles damaged, port and starboard engines shock loaded. Cat AC.

6 June 1943

Wellington III (BJ801). (F/S Swindells) disappeared into the sea off Scarborough between 1100hrs and 1800hrs while on cross country.

11/12 June 1943

Wellington III (BK 559). (Sgt Dellar) went missing from 'nickel' operation over Nantes.

15 June 1943

Wellington X (HE465) – approach made too fast. Overshot, pilot tried to swing aircraft onto perimeter but port undercarriage collapsed. No casualties. Cat AC.

19 June 1943

Wellington X (BK142). (Sgt Powell) Starboard engine failed at 300ft on take-off. Aircraft crashed and caught fire. Two of the crew injured. Category E *(i.e., a write-off)*.

21 June 1943

Wellington III (BK304). Starboard undercarriage collapsed on landing. No casualties. Cat AC.

22/23 June 1943

Sixteen aircraft were despatched to take part in four 'nickel' raids over France (Paris, Orleans, Le Mans and Rheims). Wellington X (HE527), piloted by F/S Hennessy, failed to return and the crew were all posted as missing, presumed killed in action. *(For further details see Appendix 1.)*

23/24 June 1943

Wellington X (BK 366). Made a single-engined crash landing at Wing on return from 'nickel' operation. No casualties. Cat AC.

1 July 1943

Wellington III (BK 255) crashed while trying to land at Exeter after 'nickel' raid. Flak had set the starboard engine on fire and the port engine also caught fire. All the crew were killed except rear gunner (Sgt Sheldon).

4 July 1943

Wellington (BK146). Starboard engine failed. Single-engine landing made OK and the aircraft was undamaged.

4/5 July 1943 – 0020hrs

Wellington 'L' (DF 641) overshot and crash-landed at Jurby. No casualties. The aircraft flaps, lights and W/T were all u/s and it also had engine trouble.

7 July 1943 – 0344hrs

Wellington 'U' (HE238) (F/O Beare) crashed at Newbuildings Farm near the 'Hanging Wicket' Pub (1.5 miles east of the aerodrome) on return from a 'bullseye' exercise. The aircraft dived vertically into the ground. Considered to be due to loss of control in cloud. All five crew were killed. (Pilot F/L Fenwick)

11 July 1943

Wellington (BJ 991). Port engine failed and the aircraft appeared to be going out of control. The pilot ordered crew to bale out but regained control after two had done so. Pilot then made a normal single-engine landing. One of the crew who baled out was uninjured, the other broke a small bone in his foot.

16 July 1943

Wellington (HE413). Failure of rear crankshaft roller race. Aircraft made a successful single-engine landing.

16 July 1943

Wellington (BK404). Revolutions of port engine began to drop on take-off. Brought to a stand on grass beyond end of runway. No injury or structural damage. It was later found that the armature of the constant speed unit was burnt out.

31 July 1943

Wellington 'E' (917). (Capt F/S Clifton) had to land without flaps on No. 1 Runway. Pilot unable to pull up aircraft which crashed on the railway embankment at the north (Stowe) end of the runway and burnt out. All crew escaped, the bomb aimer (Sgt Rooks) with minor injuries.

7 August 1943 – 0150hrs

Wellington 'O' from Seighford swung off runway on landing. Port undercarriage collapsed about 25 yards off runway. Crew unhurt.

11 August 1943 – 0940hrs

Wellington 'R' (F/L Metcalfe & crew) collided with Master belonging to Ternhill. There were no survivors.

11 August 1943

Wellington 'Z' from Seighford (F/Sgt Mace), in taxying round the perimeter crashed into a tractor 75 yards off the perimeter.

12 August 1943

Tomahawk (AH896) crash-landed at Lichfield. Undercarriage collapsed.

13/14 August 1943 – 0540hrs

Hixon's 'H' (pilot Sgt Bennett) called up that starboard tyre was burst. Made a daylight belly landing. Landing tee put on right of No. 2 Runway. Pilot landed to right of runway at 0645hrs. Crew unhurt. Slight fire put out.

25 August 1943

Hixon's 'O' (P/O Woodley) was struck by lightning while returning over Wales. The crew were preparing to bale out when the engine picked up again after seeming u/s so they carried on. On completing their detail over Bagot's Park, the starboard (front turret) gun suddenly fired a burst, so they returned to base at full speed. On examining the aircraft it was found that there were large rents in the fuselage and that part of the propeller was missing.

26 August 1943 – 1514hrs

A Wellington from Hixon crashed on Runway 1 at Seighford while avoiding workmen on runway when taking off. Crew uninjured. The starboard wing hit the front of a lorry and the civilian driver had a grazed leg.

1 September 1943

Wellington (HE202) 'O' (F/O Whitehead) returned on one engine. Crew told to bale out. Pilot and wireless operator told to land at Seighford on long runway. Directly afterwards Seighford's 'G' reported a fire. The aircraft crashed on Lawrence's farm between Eccleshall and Bishop Offley (Cat E). The search party of 200 found all crew safe.

(NOTE: The log doesn't make clear if the pilot and WO were safe too.)

3 September 1943

Wellington (X3564) Hixon's 'U' (Sgt Chester) crashed into cliff near Jurby. All killed.

5 September 1943

Wellington (Z1730) Hixon's 'M' crashed into the sea off Aberdeen at 0832hrs. Three of the crew picked up at about 2100 hours. Pilot (Sgt Newton) and Air Gunner (Sgt Dale) drowned.

10 September 1943

A visiting Wellington (BK 152), with six crew from No 27 OTU at Lichfield, failed to gain sufficient height on take-off from the main runway. It hit the south-east corner of Wychdon Lodge, knocking off a tower, then crashed and gouged a trench across the A51 road before bursting into flames in a field on the Western side of the road. All the crew were killed. Pilot was Frank Stringer (Australian). *(Information from fellow Australian, Ken Tweedie – navigator.)*

19 September 1943

Wellington (X3353) crash-landed at West Freugh owing to oil leakage. No injuries.

1 October 1943

Wellington III (X4002). Port engine cut out soon after take-off. Aircraft was landed without damage to aircraft or injury to crew.

2 October 1943

Wellington X (HE 471). Landed at Pershore. Two of the crew (wireless operator and bomb aimer) baled out when the aircraft iced up over Rhyl. They were never found despite a five day search.

5 October 1943

Wellington III (BK349) from Seighford. Undercarriage collapsed on normal landing. Swung off runway. No injuries or fire.

5 October 1943

Wellington (X3819) developed excessive vibration and became difficult to control. The dinghy broke loose and wrapped itself around tailplane. No crew injuries.

7 October 1943

Wellington (HF471) made normal landing but the port undercarriage collapsed.

7 October 1943

Wellington X3939 attempted a crash landing on a short runway and overshot onto the road. Crew all safe. *(Although uncertain it is assumed this was the north-south runway (16) and the plane crashed across Station (New) Road.)*

12 October 1943

Hixon's Wellington 'Q' (BK443) circled with its port engine on fire. Aircraft tried to go round again after coming in but on the second circuit it crashed one mile to the south-west, probably at Pasturefields by the Trent and Mersey Canal. The crew escaped. (Pilot Sgt McKrill.)

17 October 1943

Wellington III (BJ 971) crashed at Seighford after hitting trees at the end of the runway. Port engine cut out on take-off. No fire or injuries.

26 October 1943

Wellington Mk. X (HE 696) crashed at Burnaston. Overshot in fog and hit hangar after circling for twenty minutes. Air bomber Levene killed.

7 November 1943

Wellington 'A' (BK 821) crashed near RAF Cranage at 2145hrs. No casualties.

9 November 1943 – 0950hrs

Seighford's Wellington 'H' made belly landing, U/C collapsed. No casualties.

12 November 1943 – 1125hrs

Hixon's Wellington 'J' made a belly landing following port engine failure on take-off.

12 November 1943 – 1220hrs.

Whitley (BD 497) when ready to taxi out from dispersal received tail damage from collision with Wellington 'P'. Propellor and geodetics damaged on Wellington.

14/15 November 1943

0146hrs	Hixon Wellington 'S' crashed near Tenby due to icing. Crew baled out. *(See fascinating further detail of this accident in Chapter Five.)*
0216hrs	Seighford's Wellington 'O' crash-landed at Jurby. No casualties.
0245hrs	Seighford's Wellington 'R' overshot at Llanwrog. No casualties.

22 November 1943 – 2230hrs.

Wellington (BJ770) burst tyre on landing and swung to right. Undercarriage collapsed.

23 November 1943 – 1730hrs.

Tomahawk (AK128) ran into petrol bowser on the perimeter track. The port wing was damaged.

23 November 1943 – 2140hrs

Seighford Wellington 'O' (X3883) crashed at Hoar Cross. Pilot Sgt Collett safe but other four crew (navigator, wireless operator and two air gunners) killed.

24 November 1943 – 1537hrs

Seighford's Wellington 'A' crashed due to swing on take-off. No-one hurt.

29 November 1943

Hixon's Wellington 'G' broke undercarriage on landing. No casualties.

30 November 1943 – 1620hrs.

Oxford (P1826) belly landed at Dosthill, Tamworth. No casualties.

21 January 1944 – 1905hrs.

Hixon Wellington 'O', after concluding detail, was damaged when taxying owing to inadvertent retraction of undercarriage by pilot. No injuries.

21 January 1944 – 2220hrs

Wellington 'P' belly landed at Warmwell owing to port engine failure. The five crew had all baled out and although one injured his foot, all the crew were OK.

9 February 1944 – 1145hrs

Hixon Wellington 'V' (HE465) overshot and crash-landed.

(NOTE: Records in log book become far more general from this date with different arrangement of information.)

10 February 1944 – 1555hrs

Hixon Wellington 'K' (HE516) crashed owing to engine failure and burnt out. Sgt Welstead was badly burned and later died. Other crew escaped injury.

(See Chapter Three for description of brave attempted rescue of Sgt Welstead by local villager Cyril Fradley.)

24 February 1944 (or 4/2/44) – 2222hrs

'Bullseye' operation. One aircraft (HE 903) crashed at Seighford/Ranton. All crew killed.

5 March 1944 – 1130hrs

Tomahawk (AH 850) made a successful glide landing at Condover after engine failure.

5 March 1944 – 1405hrs

Martinet 'O' crash-landed at Hinstock. The pilot was OK. The engine cut out at 3,000ft.

7 March 1944 – 2000hrs

Seighford Wellington 'S' landed with burst starboard tyre. All OK.

11 March 1944 – 1140hrs

Tomahawk 'K' (AH832) crashed on the railway on take-off. Pilot F/O Chapman was OK.

18 March 1944 – 0045hrs

Wellington 'O' landed at Topcliffe owing to weather. Overshot runway and sustained some damage.

25 March 1944

Seighford Wellington 'W' Heavy landing and bounced. Pilot retracted undercarriage and attempted to regain circuit. Aircraft stalled and made belly landing on runway. Crew unhurt.

11 April 1944 – 2100hrs

Hixon Wellington 'G' (HF 471) crashed at Fandhad Farm near Skelton, Yorks (Ref WA 233425). Crew (6) all killed. (Pilot F/S C H Gale.)

14 April 1944

Tomahawk 'E' (AH926) crash-landed at Peplow. The undercarriage collapsed on touching down. Pilot unhurt.

15 April 1944 – 0010hrs

Wellington 'D' (HE 465). (Pilot F/L Bull) crashed near Swansmoor/Newton (ref 485457) immediately after take-off and burst into flames on impact. All crew (five) killed.

20 April 1944

0945hrs   Wellington 'J' (HE 507). Port tyre burst while taxying along perimeter and the port undercarriage collapsed immediately after.

1030hrs   Wellington 'U' (LN 590) made good landing but brakes failed to hold and ran onto railway line beyond No.1 Runway end.

21 April 1944 – 1700hrs

Wellington 'Q' (BK347) (Pilot F/O Barrett) crashed on mountain side, at Whernside (O/S 98 Ref: 743817) when 150 miles off-course on a navigational exercise. Rear Gunner Sgt Marks survived with minor injuries. Remainder of crew (six) all killed. Aircraft complete wreck.

(Note: This is the first aircraft in the line-up of Wellingtons on the well-known photograph and painting of the airfield – as used on front cover of this book.)

23 April 1944 – 2130hrs

Wellington 'D' (DF 612). (Pilot F/Officer Etherton) made a successful emergency landing. Port engine partially u/s.

26 April 1944 – 0133hrs

Wellington 'P' (DF640). (Pilot F/O N A Mousdell) crashed after overshoot (Runway 279) on Weston Bank (ref K417474). Crew of three were all killed. Aircraft caught fire after striking ground.

3 May 1944 – 1229hrs

Wellington 'O' (DF622) crashed on approach to No. 2 Runway. Crew all safe.

5 May 1944 – 2340hrs

Wellington 'S' (BJ821) made a forced landing at Sleap owing to starboard engine failure. Four crew baled out successfully and pilot made a successful landing.

9 May 1944

Wellington 'T' (HE 413) (Pilot F/L Thorne) failed to return from 'nickel' raid.

9 May 1944 – 2325hrs.

Wellington 'L' (LN533) returned early from 'nickel' with intercom trouble. Approached normally but burst into flames on touch down. Fire extinguished quickly. No injuries.

15 May 1944 – 2359hrs

Wellington 'A' (MF114) (S/Ldr Swann) made a successful emergency flapless landing. Hydraulics u/s.

16 May 1944 – 1525hrs

Wellington 'M (LN 712)'. Port engine failure. Perfect belly landing. Crew OK.

27 May 1944

One of eight Wellington aircraft on 'Bullseye' 'T' (DF641) crashed at a spot 5 miles SW of Ingham. Crew of seven all killed (pilot F/Sgt Kutter).

31 May 1944

One of eight aircraft on 'nickel' raid, Wellington 'O' (BJ597) couldn't maintain height due to engine trouble and crashed near Keevil at 0145hrs. Crew all baled out safely. (Pilot F/O Boullier).

10 June 1944 – 1116hrs.

Wellington 'H' (HE820). (Pilot F/L MacLean) made a low overshoot at Seighford and banked sharply to port and crashed just off the airfield. Pilot and Air Bomber Sgt Kelly killed. Other two members of crew safe.

24 June 1944 – 0125hrs.

Wellington 'W' (HE858) Pilot F/O Gray landed with burst port tyre. Pilot did not know which tyre had burst and when landing jettisoned fuel and instructed crew to take up crash positions. Made good landing and crew all OK.

16 July 1944 – 0135hrs.

Seighford Wellington 'Y' (NC678) (Pilot F/S Philips) caught fire in the air. Crew ordered to bale out and aircraft the crashed at map ref. VK184539, 2 miles from Cannock. Four crew killed. Aircraft burnt out.

16 July 1944 – 2250hrs.

Wellington 'R' (HF802) landed without calling on R/T. Made late touchdown, with 'speed very high'. Failed to stop on perimeter, crossed railway line and stopped in field just beyond railway. Crew OK.

18 July 1944 – 0056hrs.

Wellington 'E' (BK443) crash-landed (belly landing) at Coltishall after port engine caught fire 60 miles out to sea. Undercarriage would not come down even with emergency bottle. Crew OK.

23 July 1944

0020hrs   Wellington 'D' (X4002) crashed near Wymondham after port engine failure on 'bullseye' mission. Crew baled out. All OK. Aircraft burnt out.

0035hrs   Wellington 'T' (X4003) (F/O Grant) could not pull up after landing, crossed perimeter and the railway, causing damage to aircraft.

24 July 1944 – 1745hrs

Fire broke out in Wellington 'R' (HF 727) while in dispersal forty-five minutes. after it had landed from cross-country flight. Every effort immediately made to put fire out but without success. Aircraft completely destroyed.

4 August 1944 – 2353hrs

Wellington 'P' (HE 525) from Seighford landed on diversion instructions. Overshot runway and the port wheel collapsed. Crew OK.

8 August 1944 – 1005hrs

Wellington 'Y' (LN588). Undercarriage collapsed when swung to starboard off runway onto perimeter. Crew OK.

9 August 1944 – 0200hrs

Wellington 'H' (HE413). Aircraft swung to port on touching down, port undercarriage collapsed – port tyre burst. Crew OK.

9 August 1944 – 0215hrs.

Wellington 'E' (HE828) crashed at Yeovilton on a 'nickel' raid. Had been hit by enemy flak. Crew baled out and were OK.

11 August 1944 – 1515hrs

Wellington 'T' (DF612) heavy landing, starboard engine failed. Crew OK.

(See Chapter Five for first-hand account of this accident by Noel Burton.)

12 August 1944

Wellington 'R' (BK 562) (F/O Clifton). Instrument failure (artificial horizon and directional Gyro). Crew were ordered to bale out. Two members of crew OK, two injured, three dead (pupil pilot and two air gunners). Crashed at North Wilford, near Nottingham.

(Note – There were various emergency landings during August 1944 but without casualties.)

26 August 1944

1500hrs   Wellington 'Z' (LP570) P/O Mettrick. Overshot runway and ran onto railway Crew OK. Undercart damaged.

2255hrs   Wellington 'E' (HE828) F/Sgt George – overshot runway and also ran onto railway. Crew OK.

30 August 1944 – 1725hrs

Wellington 'U' (ME999) made a belly landing when pilot deliberately retracted the undercarriage because he was overshooting. Crew OK.

27 September 1944 – 1930hrs

Wellington 'E' (BJ799). Port engine cut on take-off, over-ran runway.

1 October 1944 – 2310hrs

Wellington 'K' (BK 297). Successful emergency landing with starboard propellor u/s and flaps u/s

12 October 1944

Wellington (MF698). Aircraft failed to return from cross-country (F/S White) flight. Crew presumed killed. Last contact by W/T at 0338

14 October 1944 – 1916hrs

Wellington 'B' (LN 645) landed with undercarriage retracted. Crew OK.

16 October 1944 – 2150hrs

Wellington 'P' (X3356) (Pilot F/S Vallender) Aircraft on cross country was seen to crash at Ingestre Park. Aircraft burnt out. Crew of six all killed. Last W/T contact at 2141hrs

21 October 1944 – 1825hrs

F/O Brogan (Screened Instructor Pilot) and pupil pilot Barrated of Wellington 'N' (LP616) retracted undercarriage instead of flaps after landing. Crew OK and aircraft only superficially damaged.

25 October 1944 – 1453hrs

Hurricane 'P' (LF170) from Hixon with Pilot F/O Browne. Aircraft struck a tree at Seighford. Part of wing broke away and aircraft crashed into the ground near the officers' mess. A/C was a total wreck and the pilot killed.

27 October 1944

Wellington 'A' (BK 146). Starboard engine failed on take-off. Over-ran runway and aircraft caught fire. Crew OK but the aircraft u/s.

20 November 1944 – 1124hrs

Wellington (LP569) caught fire in Hangar. No cause apparent. Aircraft u/s

(See Chapter Four for details.)

30 November 1944 – 2000hrs

Wellington 'K' (LP616) F/O Laurie called up on R/T 'port engine failure'. Made a single-engine landing but overshot runway and crossed railway line. Crew all OK.

8 January 1945

1130hrs   Wellington (LN166) 'G' (Pilot F/S M F MacLean) crashed at (K305492) Burton's Lane near Eccleshall. Crew (six) all killed.

1416hrs   Wellington 'B' (NC731) (F/S Lewis). Last contact at 1416hrs position 5153N 0443W. 'Passed by Bristol and ack by aircraft'. Aircraft and crew presumed lost.

14 January 1945

1808hrs   'Sweepstake' mission with twelve aircraft airborne.

(This was an operation to divert German fighter aircraft away from the main attacking RAF force.)

15 January 1945

0046hrs   Wellington 'A' (LP828) Pilot F/O Hickman. Diverted and ran short of fuel. Crew baled out. Aircraft crashed near Nottingham.

0020hrs   Wellington 'M' (LP830) Pilot Sgt. Hudson. Also diverted and ran short of fuel. Crashed near Ruddington. Crew baled out and again OK.

(Final entry as No. 30 OTU at Hixon.)

Acknowledgements

This book could not have been produced without the willing help and support of many people. In particular I must thank those who, in the 1990s, allowed me to interview them and record their experiences. Sadly, with the passage of time, many will have passed away, but I hope this record of their memories will be of interest to many others and help preserve their experiences for future generations.

Interviews / Contacts

Fred Shufflebotham	Stoke	Construction Contractor
Mrs Dorothy Jenkinson	Hixon Resident	
Joe Tinker	Hixon Resident	
Cyril Fradley BEM	Hixon Resident	
Bill Chellingworth	Gnosall	Electrician
Mr Charlie Morrall		Joiner
Ron Cull	Sheffield	Aircraft Recovery Team
David Starey	Stone	Leading Aircraftman (Mainframes)
Flt Sgt Stan Botwright	Woking	Physical Training Instructor
John (Jack) Weaver	Little Haywood	Electrical Engineer (Construction)
Betty Jermy	(Rugeley)	LACW Fitter 2E
Mrs E Clark	Stafford	Friend of Betty Jermy
Mrs Kate Perry	Keyworth	Wireless Operator, Signals Section
Mr W E Harper	Thorpe St Andrew	Fitter Bomb Armourer
Deryck (Jack) Brew	Burntwood	Corporal Armourer
Sgt Norman Lowe	Bolton	Sgt Armourer Fitter
Flt Lt, Steve Boylan	Stoke	Pilot Instructor
Flt Sgt Ken Stott	Welshpool	Navigator
Cliff Michelmore CBE	Reigate	Engineer Officer
George Riley	Stafford	Aerial Photography Instructor
Sgt A (Bert) Blaydon	Leyton	Air Gunner
Sgt John Cooper	Stafford	Air Gunner
Flt Lt Bill Hickox DFC	Castle Donnington	Navigation Instructor
P/O Bryce Chase	Canada	Pilot
Flt Sgt Ken Tweedie	Queensland, Australia	Navigator/Instructor
Sgt David Fellows	Haywoods Heath	Rear Gunner
Flt Sgt Noel Burton DFM	South Africa	Pilot/Instructor
Mrs Diana Calderwood	Berkhamsted	Daughter of Noel Burton
Flt Sgt Terry Hillyer	Croydon	Air Gunner
Flt Sgt Jim Syratt	Henley in Arden	Navigator
Evelyn & Olive Jones	Stafford	Wartime Hixon Residents

P/O W A (Bill) Gourlay DFC	Tasmania	Navigator
Robyn Conn	Tasmania	Daughter of Bill Gourlay
Judy Leader (nee Rowse)	New Zealand	Daughter of Sgt Deryck Rowse
Archie Anderson	New Zealand	Aviation Historian
Marshall Boylan	Leek	Aviation Historian – Son of Flt/Lt Steve Boylan
John Teasdale	Stafford	Aircraft Observer and Artist
Rob Brittlebank	Stafford	Aviation Historian
Tom Renshaw	Banstead	Relative of Les Freeman (Pilot)
Dr Stephen Collier		Local Pilot/Photographer

References

In the Thick of it   (1994)   SQD LDR Ralph Edwards DSO
Images Publishing (Malvern)

RAF Moreton in Marsh   (1995)   J H Hamlin & G V Tyack
E P Lowe Ltd (Broadway)

Wellington in Action   (1986)   Ron Mackay
Squadron/Signal Publications (Texas)

Wellington Special   (1974)   Alec Lumsden
Ian Allan Ltd (London)

The Means of Victory   (1992)   Bomber Command
Charterhouse Publications Ltd

Staffordshire Airfields in the Second World War (2007)   Martyn Chorlton
Countryside Books (Newbury)

The Loch Ness Wellington (1986)   Stephen Flower
After the Battle No 53
Battle of Britain Prints (London)

Rewards of the Years, One Man's Story (1987)   W A (Bill) Gourlay DFC
Launceston, Australia

Bomber Boys   (2007)   Patrick Bishop
Harper Perennial (London)

About the Author

Dr Malcolm Garner B.Ed, Ph.D

Malcolm Garner lived in Hixon from 1987 to 2007 and it was during this period that he became interested in the history of the village and in the things for which it is known and remembered, not only by locals but also by many others around the world.

He was a founding member of Hixon Local History Society and acted as its first chairman for more than a decade while living in the village. As well as his interest in RAF Hixon he also undertook considerable research in, and gives talks about, the Hixon Level Crossing Rail Disaster of January 1968, in which eleven people lost their lives. He also edited and published the fascinating and detailed written memories of the late Eddie Craik, whose father had been the village policeman in the early 1930s. These were published in 2002 under the title of *Memories of Hixon*.

Malcolm trained as a teacher and teacher of the deaf, and from 1987 to 2000 was Head of Staffordshire's Education Support Services for children who were deaf, visually impaired or blind, or had physical disability. Malcolm retired in 2007, his final position being head of Special Education Support Services in Birmingham.

In 2004, three years before he retired, Malcolm visited Gambia in West Africa and, finding very limited specialist educational provision in the country, established the 'Gambian Deaf Children's Support Project' charity to help develop education, social and health services for deaf children and adults in the country. He has continued this work after retirement, visiting Gambian nearly thirty times over the course of the past fifteen years.

Malcolm has also continued his lifelong interest in railways and is a regular driver at the Amerton Railway near Hixon. He also volunteers with Southern Locomotives Ltd, helping to restore and maintain main line steam locomotives in Birmingham and Swanage.

He has three children and six grandchildren and now lives in Bewdley in Worcestershire.